Basic How-To's

I like to choose a basic all-over design paper for the background.

Then I use a decorative paper with great images to tear or cut out accents for embellishments on pages.

1. Select a background paper and an accent paper.

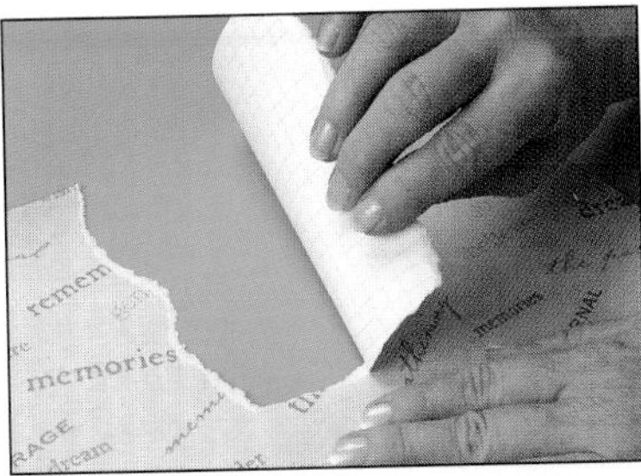

2. Tear or cut accent paper.

3. Age the edges with chalk.

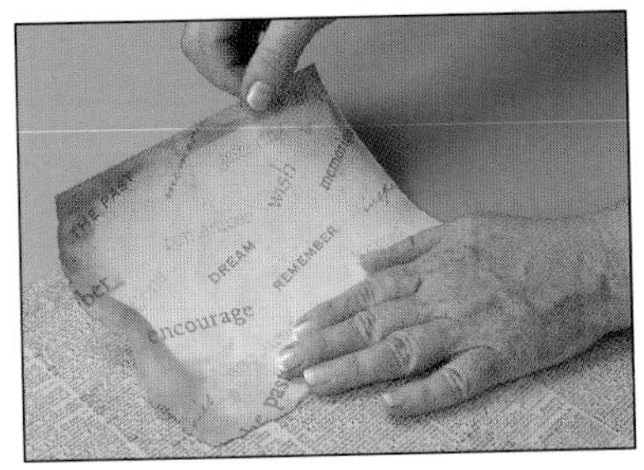

4. Adhere to page.

5. Add photos, paper accents and embellishments.

Torn out words.

Transparency word.

Stamp in clay.

Aged tag with eyelet.

FRIENDSHIP *by Renée Plains*

MATERIALS: *Design Originals* Legacy Collage Papers (#0547 Dictionary, #0551 Legacy Words) • *Design Originals* Transparency Sheet (#0556 Word Tags) • 2" x 2" Black slide mount • *Hero Arts* script rubber stamp • *Staz-On* metallic Bronze ink pad • *My Mind's Eye* "Old is New" Ceiling Tile frame and tile clip • 3 aged metal-rimmed circle tags • Eyelets • *Anima Designs* Copper and aluminum tags • *Making Memories* 'Friendship' definition sticker • Punches (1/2", 1" heart) • Polymer clay • Pop Dots • Black marker • 'No 5' stamped on oval polymer clay and baked according to package directions, then aged with brown acrylic paint

INSTRUCTIONS: Tear a strip of Legacy Words paper, chalk edges to age then glue in place. • Glue picture in frame and place on page; glue ceiling tile clip to page. • Attach Copper tag to frame with eyelets. • Stamp 'No. 5' on oval polymer clay and bake as manufacturer directs, then age with Brown acrylic paint. Glue to Copper tag. • Insert transparency in slide mount stamped with script. • Cut words from Legacy Words paper and glue on frame and on page. • Punch a heart from Copper, punch a hole in heart and page and set eyelet to hold in place. • Place "Friendship" sticker on page. • Set tags on page with eyelets. • Adhere remaining objects on page.

1. Ink a rubber stamp with Cat's Eye fluid chalk or an archival ink.

2. Press stamp onto a slide mount. Color edges with a black marker.

3. Insert a transparency in mount. Attach mount to page with Pop Dots.

REMINISCE *by Renée Plains*
MATERIALS: *Design Originals* Legacy Collage Papers (#0530 Mom's Sewing Box, #0533 Dress Patterns) • Photo of couple and photo booth strip • *EK Success* Rebecca Sower Antique Roses stickers • *Making Memories* 'reminisce' definition sticker • Buttons • Thread spool labels • *Rubbermoon* 'remembering' rubber stamp • Chalk
INSTRUCTIONS: Make frame with oval opening from Mom's Sewing Box paper. • Glue elements on page. • Chalk to age as desired.

Preserving Treasures

When choosing albums, paper and accents for a scrapbook, make sure everything is archival safe. Unsafe items will accelerate the aging of photos. Look for albums and materials that do NOT contain PVC. PVC releases gas that causes photos to yellow. Photos may also become sticky and difficult or impossible to remove with time.

Avoid paper containing acid. Acid migrates and causes the paper itself to deteriorate which will affect your photos and memorabilia. It is best to use paper that is buffered. Buffered paper will prevent the paper from becoming acidic. Avoid lignin, the substance that holds wood cells together. If your paper contains lignin, it browns with age, crumbles and disintegrates!

It is best to use a photo-safe, acid-free adhesive made for scrapbooks. I like Aleene's Memory Glue as an adhesive for paper and memorabilia. It dries slowly so you can reposition an item and comes packaged with both a fine point tip and a brush tip, that is great for spreading a thin layer of glue. I use a tape runner or photo splits to secure photos. These clear tapes minimize the damage to my album if I need to remove a photo after time. Foam dots give items instant dimension.

Storing Your Treasures

Safe storage of your keepsakes is of utmost importance. Photos need to be in a stable environment. Temperature and humidity affect photographs and documents more than any other element. The best temperature is less than 70°F, with the relative humidity under 50%.

It's best to store albums upright, in a cool dry place. Do not position a bumpy object directly opposite a photo on the facing page, as damage can occur. Following these recommendations takes a bit of planning, but the end results are worth it.

Collage Elements

Collage encompasses both art and craft. One of the most expressive and versatile art forms, it lends itself to many different applications - altered books, cards, framed art, 3-D sculptures, and more recently... scrapbooks! It's so fun to pull out all the stops and engage in such a freeform style of scrapbooking. Inspiration is found within your photos, the rest is up to you!

Many scrapbook enthusiasts are a bit tired of 'cookie cutter' scrapbook pages. They have found that there is more to designing an album page than lining up four square photos in the middle of a piece of cardstock. Design Originals has created a wonderful line of collage papers with a vintage feel. Unique supplies and found objects are available that can be added to pages quickly and easily.

Adding embellishments has become a hot trend among scrappers! There's a fine art to adding just the right amount of 'goodies' without overwhelming the focal point, which is... the photos, of course! Allow your imagination to run free as you absorb the phenomenal pages of this book. Use our projects for inspiration to make your album a personal expression of love.

PROFILES OF POLAND

by Carol Wingert

MATERIALS: *Design Originals* Legacy Collage Paper (#0553 Map) • Cardstock (Ivory, Light Green) • *Lazertran* Ink Jet transfer paper • *7 gypsies* waxed linen • *Ellison* Tag die-cut • *NRN Designs* stickers • Postage stamps • *3M* ink jet acetate transparency • *Plaid* Matte Mod Podge • PVA glue

INSTRUCTIONS: Scan photos and copy onto Lazertran ink jet transfer paper. • Follow the manufacturer's directions. • Apply transfer to aged and torn cardstock coated with PVA glue. • Brayer so that wrinkles and air bubbles are removed. • When dry, coat with a layer of matte Mod Podge for protection. • Computer generate title (I used the Double Arc option in Print Artist). • Print onto ink jet transparency. Set aside to dry. • Tear and age Map paper and adhere to top of layout. • Cut out title and adhere to map. • Position aged stamps and stickers on map paper and adhere in place. • Adhere photo panel to bottom of layout. • Hand-stitch sections together with waxed linen. • Add tag with handwritten journaling.

BOYS WILL BE BOYS

by Carol Wingert

MATERIALS: *Design Originals* Legacy Collage Paper (#0540 Skates) • Cardstock (Tan, Brown) • *3M* ink jet acetate transparency • *7 gypsies* Walnut ink and typewriter key frames • *Limited Edition* Typewriter alphabet rubber stamps • Twill Tape (fabric stores) • *American Tag* brads • *Amaco* Crafting Copper • *Chemtek* Patina aging solution • Hemp

INSTRUCTIONS: Scan photo and print onto ink jet transparency. Adhere to a cardstock mat. (The color of the cardstock will show through the clear and light parts of the transparency). • Age twill tape with walnut ink. When dry, print computer generated letters onto twill tape. • Wrap twill tape around mat and secure on the back with tape. • Stamp typewriter letters onto scrap cardstock, cut out and frame in round typewriter key frames. • Lay hemp under each frame and secure frames to photo mat on all four corners. • Adhere photo, mat and collage paper to layout. • Cut strips of Copper; age with Chemtek Patina solution according to manufacturer's directions. • Create folded metal tabs on all four sides of the layout and secure with antique Copper mini brads.

SISTERHOOD *by Carol Wingert*

MATERIALS: *Design Originals* Legacy Collage Paper (#0530 Mom's Sewing Box) • Cream cardstock • *Manto Fev* vintage slide mounts • *Memory Lane* Square frame studs & ribbon • *Stampers Anonymous* Alphabet rubber stamps • *Ranger* Adirondack Aging and Stamping ink • *My Weakness* charm

INSTRUCTIONS: Crop photos to fit into vintage slide mounts and insert. • Print saying on computer; cut into strips and position on layout. • Add collage papers. • Sponge on dye ink to age. • Add ribbon, tiny frame studs and charm. • Stamp 2nd generation image of letters to create word "Sisters" on the collage paper.

Booklet Pages 1 & 2 - Include family photos and memorabilia.

Booklet Pages 3 & 4 - Highlight several generations in your book.

Collecting Treasures

Over the years my collection of keepsakes has grown. I'm sure I'm not the only mom that saved every school paper, art project and award my kids brought home. Then there were unique little goodies I snatched up from special occasions such as a Flintstone napkin from my little sister's 3rd birthday party and the origami frog my big sister made for me as a young teen. These items are a great part of my life that I like to reminisce about as I thumb through my albums.

Preserving Memories

The past ten years have taught me how to preserve my memories in safe and artistic ways. By using archival paper, adhesives and embellishments, my memorabilia is sure to look as good many years from now as it did when I collected it! My kids, grandkids and future generations will enjoy moments from the past as they browse through my scrapbooks and read journaling I wrote about photos and the facts behind them. Because I've taken the time and effort to create eye-catching collage pages, there is little chance that they'll get bored looking through our family albums!

Designing Altered Style Pages

When I sit down with a stack of photos, I spread them out in front of me and take a good long look. I consider the theme, story or event, colors, shapes and even the textures present in the images. Then I select the best shots to add to my scrapbook and safely store the others. As I create the layout in my head, I make sure my chosen papers and collage elements enhance the photos and bring them to life!

For instance, if there is a lot of action in the photo, I make sure that this energy is carried over in my layout and accent shapes ('Swimming Lessons', page 32). I often echo a focal point or detail in a photo to add to the charm (shaker box pool rope and floating board accents). On the other hand, if the event is a classy night out ('Prom Night', page 31), I keep the colors simple and use elegant embellishments.

The mood of the event is also important to note. I remember the night of my daughter's high school talent show, when she sang a song she had written. She created an almost folksy atmosphere as she strummed her guitar and sang. For this layout (page 11), I pulled the warm colors from her dress, guitar and the stage. I added a whimsical touch with bingo accents as it was a fun school activity night!

Adding Textures

Shapes and texture play a large part in design. It is good design practice to mimic shapes, using round embellishments with a photo that has bubbles or polka dots on a person's clothing. Texture doesn't always have to be rough. In the case of "Swimming Lessons' (page 32), I echoed the smooth pool railing arch shape by including some untextured sleek metal frames.

Placement of Photos

Strategic placement of photos creates a layout that is pleasing to the eye. Notice how the square photo in the shadow box on page 32 is more interesting off to one side, than if it were simply centered. And choosing a 'stair step' photo pattern (page 11) or placing photos within an imaginary triangle boundary (page 31) adds excitement to the design. Experiment with placement of your photos and elements to produce just the right look.

Booklet Pages 5 & 6 - Include photos from a family trip.

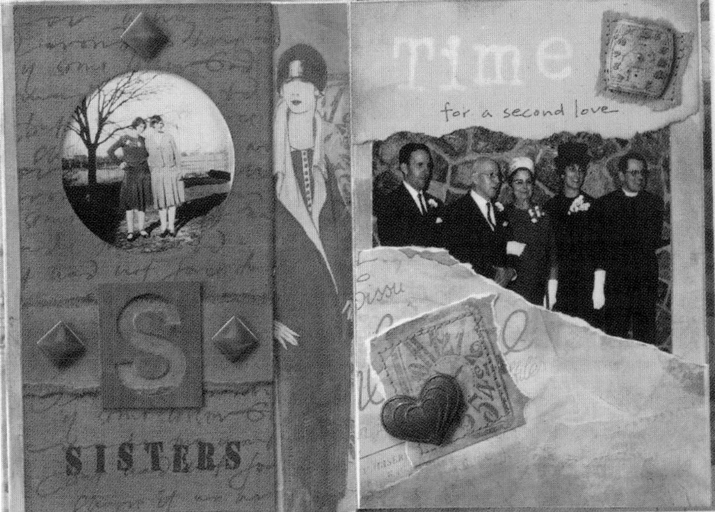

Booklet Pages 7 & 8 - Show photos from a special event.

Importance of Color

Color can make or break a layout. Legacy Collage papers come in fabulous muted colors... color, sepia tone and black and white photos all look great on these papers. I usually use shades from the photo colors instead of trying to match them exactly. I also use complementary colors. If the photo is light nearest the edge, I go with a dark background. The tiniest of details in a photo can pop, when a variation of that color is used in the background. It draws the eye right to it.

Shirley Rufener

Booklet Cover

Create a Nostalgic Keepsake Booklet!

Terrific Tip • Determine the size and number of panels needed. An even number allows the book to lay flat when open. Page size determines the size needed to create the insert. Use 12" x 12" cardstock.

FAMILY TIES BOOKLET *by Carol Wingert*

MATERIALS: *Design Originals* Legacy Collage Papers (#0526 Two Ladies, #0539 Plaid Hanky, #0542 Farm House, #0543 Brushes, #0548 Passport, #0549 Shorthand, #0551 Legacy Words) • Cream cardstock • *Books by Hand* book kit • *American Tag* eyelets • *Creative Papers Online* Lokta string • *Stampers Anonymous* vintage optical lens • *Ellison* die-cuts (negative images of numbers & letters) • *Making Memories* eyelet brads, eyelet letters, word definition sheets • *Memory Lane* hat pin • *Anima Designs* watch face and heart charm • *EK Success* Rebecca Sower Designs Mini Tag Letters • *Details* Family framed charm • *NRN Designs* butterfly sticker • Rubber stamps (*Judi-Kins, A Stamp in the Hand, Green Pepper Press, Ma Vinci's Reliquary*) • *Scrapworks* mini silver frame • *Scrapbook Interiors* scrapbook nails and wall border • *Ranger* Adirondack aging and stamping inks • *ColorBox* chalk inks • *Hillcreek Designs* button/linen thread

INSTRUCTIONS: Cover front and back covers with collage paper. • Adhere accordion fold insert pages to insides of both covers. • Cover pages with ink and various coordinating collage papers. • Add photos, lettering and embellishments. • Treat each page as though it is an individual scrapbook page done in smaller scale. • Create a "binder slip" out of corrugated paper and collage paper. • Set eyelets on each side and tie with Lokta string. • Add optical lens which has computer generated title adhered to the back of it.

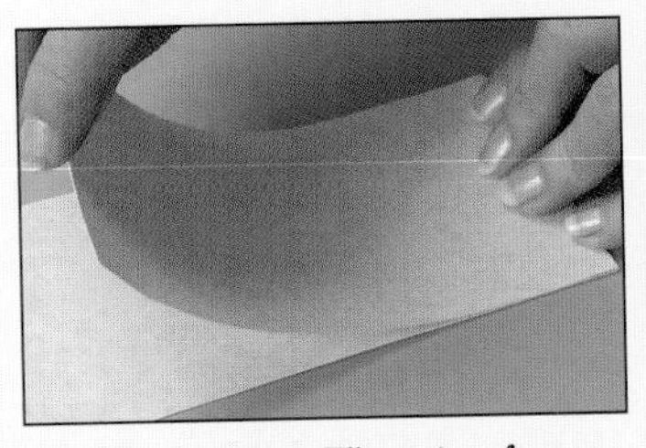

1. Cut a 40" x 7" strip for an 8-panel fold (5" x 7" panels). Fold strip in half, burnish fold with a bone folder.

2. Fold each panel in half again, toward the valley centerfold. Burnish after each fold.

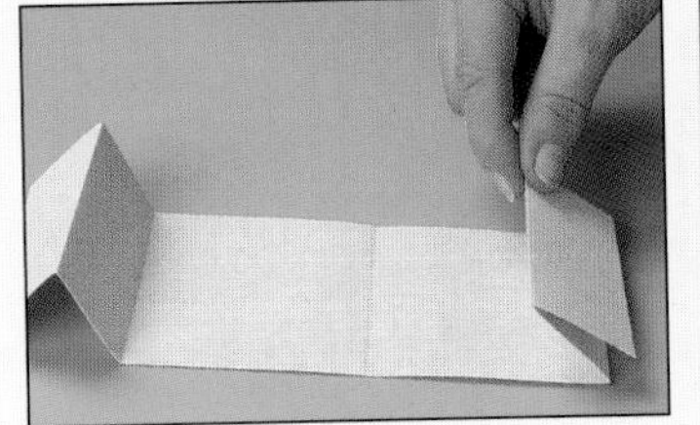

3. Fold the top panels back to the end mountain folds.

4. Fold the last sections back to the center fold.

All you need are a few photos to create a swing booklet filled with wonderful memories. This is the perfect format for a 'Random Memories' album, a 'Thank You' gift or a 'Favorite Photos' collection. Make one for all the special people in your life.

MEMORIES 'SWING BOOKLET'

by Susan Keuter

MATERIALS: *Design Originals* Legacy Collage Papers (#0531 Ladies with Hats, #0534 Ruth's Violets, #0535 Ruth's Letter, #0550 TeaDye Script, #0551 Legacy Words, #0552 Travels) • Scraps of decorative paper • Cardstock (Tan, Peach, Forest Green, Light Blue, Red) • Miscellaneous stickers • Post and screw • Twine • Flat embellishments • Eyelets • Office supply hole reinforcements • Material for template

INSTRUCTIONS: Using the template, cut out pages and punch a hole in each page. • Design your pages unassembled from the post fastener. • Punch holes in each page, reinforce.• If desired, stain hole reinforcers with ink pads before applying. • Use scraps of your favorite Legacy Collage papers and cardstock. • Mat photos and attach to pages. • Add journaling, letters and stickers. • Embellish with relatively flat items to prevent snagging when the book is opened.

Design the cover with stitching and found objects.

Create a Clever 'Swing Booklet' to Hold Photos and Memories!

Page 1 - Add a family photo, journaling and embellishments.

Page 2 - Add another family photo and priceless memories.

Page 3 - Attach a photo of the family and a key to the heart.

Helpful Hints and Tips

- It is easiest to design swing book pages first, then assemble them together. It is very important to keep in mind that the top ½" of each page will not show. It will be covered by the other pages. To help, use your template. Rotate it 180° and paper clip it over the top of each page, aligning the holes. This prevents you from placing design elements too high on the page.
- If you make your template from heavy cardstock or chipboard, it will last a long time. Cut your material 6" x 6". Punch a hole, the size of the post you intend to use, 3" from the left edge and ½" down from the top edge.
- A good size for a swing book is 6" x 6". It is small enough to carry with you and it is small enough to utilize scraps of your favorite materials from other projects.

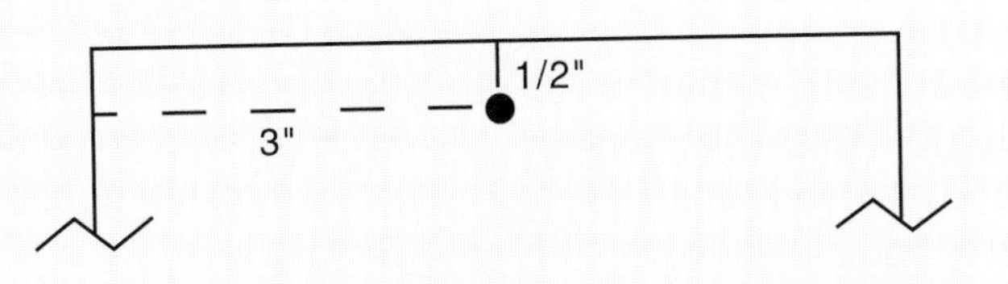

Page 4 - Embellish with a memory of a favorite pet.

Page 5 - Stitch a title for a photo of favorite children.

Use Glass Nuggets to Enlarge Small Photos, Stamped Images, an Entire Word or the First Letter in a Word!

The collage journal cover began with my favorite image from 'Two Ladies' scrapbook paper. I love this image because it reminded me of an East Indian Empress from the 16th century that I was reading about. She inspired this cover. The collage grew around her romantic face.

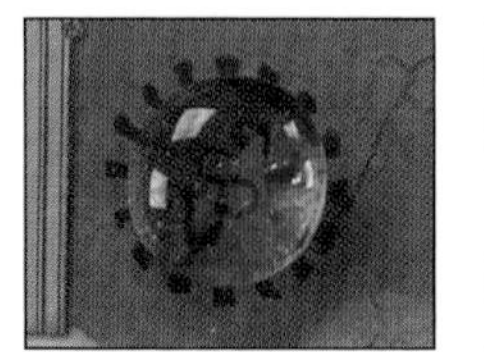
Highlight an interesting image.

Highlight an old postmark.

MEMORIES OF MEHRUNISSA *by Mary Kaye Seckler*

MATERIALS: *Design Originals* Legacy Collage Paper (#0526 Two Ladies) • *7 Gypsies* blank gatefold journal & 4 photo corners • Rubber stamps (*Treasure Cay* #282; *Missing Link* oval postmark; *Tin Can Mail* postmark cancellation; *Acey Deucy* writing stamp; *Stampington* One Man Show) • *Ranger Adirondack* Ginger ink pad • *Tsukineko StazOn* Black ink • *ColorBox Cat's Eye* Terra Cotta • Brass stencil • 2 brass latches • 8 brass brads • 1 piece negative film • Various collage materials • Gem Tac glue • Clear glass nuggets

INSTRUCTIONS: Remove covers from spirals. • Recover with papers. • Tear image from Two Ladies paper, age with Terra Cotta ink. • Position and adhere images on book cover. • Adhere stencil with Gem Tac. • Attach brass latches with brass brads.

Glass Nuggets

Glass nuggets add a touch of whimsy to pages! Nuggets are flat backed glass marbles. By placing them over tiny photos or motifs on a page, you can magnify and showcase them in a unique way.

1. Cut the photo or image slightly larger than a nugget. If possible seal both sides of the paper with Instant Decoupage.

2. Spread a very thin layer of 7800 adhesive on the back of a nugget.

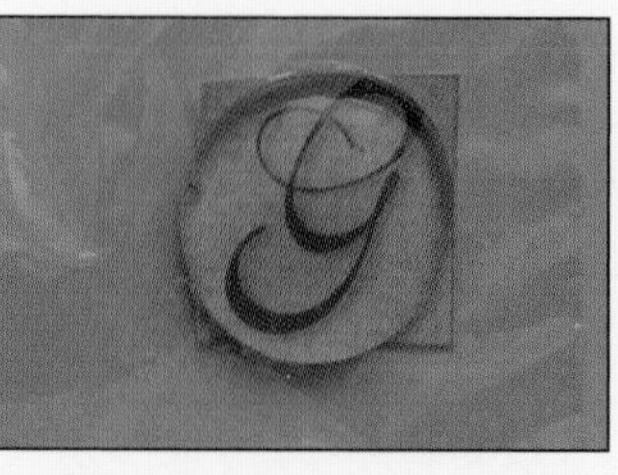

3. Place image on plastic. Press nugget firmly to push out the bubbles.

4. Allow to dry completely then peel from plastic. Trim edge and secure to project with *Aleene's* Memory Glue.

Keeping special memorabilia and photos in a scrapbook is not a new idea. The term acid-free was virtually non-existent even 20 years ago. Still, many albums were created with precious memories of days gone by. Now you can add this new creative style and protect your special photos at the same time. What fun!

Highlight the first letters of a word.

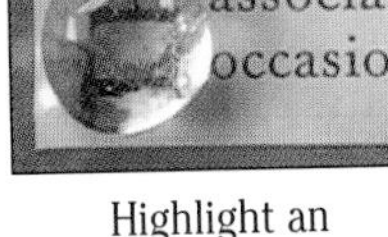

Highlight an interesting word.

YANKEETOWN SCHOOL

by Renée Plains

MATERIALS: *Design Originals* Legacy Collage Paper (#0542 Farm House, #0492 Coffee floral) • Vintage school photo • *Making Memories* 'tradition' definition sticker • *EK Success* Nostalgiques by Rebecca Sower ruler sticker • Star nailhead • Old button card • 4 Clear glass nuggets • Chalk

INSTRUCTIONS: Tear Farm House paper and glue on Coffee floral page. • Glue photo on page. • Type words, cut apart, glue in place and age with chalk. • Glue elements on page. • Age with chalk as desired.

Highlight numbers.

Highlight single letters.

JOY CAN SING *by Shirley Rufener*

MATERIALS: *Design Originals* Legacy Collage Papers (#0542 Farm House, #0544 Bingo, #0481 Teal linen, #0490 Coffee linen, #0496 TeaDye alphabet) • White vellum • *Aleene's* Memory glue & 7800 adhesive • *Xyron* 510 machine with permanent adhesive • *K & S Metals* 36-gauge Copper tooling foil • *Sizzix* die-cutter (Circles die #38-0305) • *Leather Factory* Leather alphabet stamp set • *EK Success* Block Upper Letter "O" Paper Shaper punch (#PSM15CS) • *Tsukineko StazOn* ink pads (Jet Black, Timber Brown) • 1/16" hole punch • 4 large and 4 small clear glass nuggets • 3 gold music note metal charms • Brown carpet thread • Large sewing needle • Adhesive foam dots

INSTRUCTIONS: Secure a 1 1/4" strip of edge design from TeaDye Alphabet paper to a 1 3/4" strip of Bingo paper. • Mark and pierce holes 1/2" apart, whip stitch left paper edge. Secure to scrapbook page then stitch right edge. • Secure "JOY" letters and oval plates with foam dots. • Make a vellum tag and 3 ovals from Copper foil. Stamp letters and antique. • Back large nuggets with alphabet paper and secure to page • Glue small nuggets over bingo numbers. • Tie tag to mat and adhere to page. • Glue metal charms with 7800 adhesive.

Accordion Booklet

It is simple to make a clever little booklet to hold memories of a special trip.

1. Glue glass nugget to front of camera die-cut.

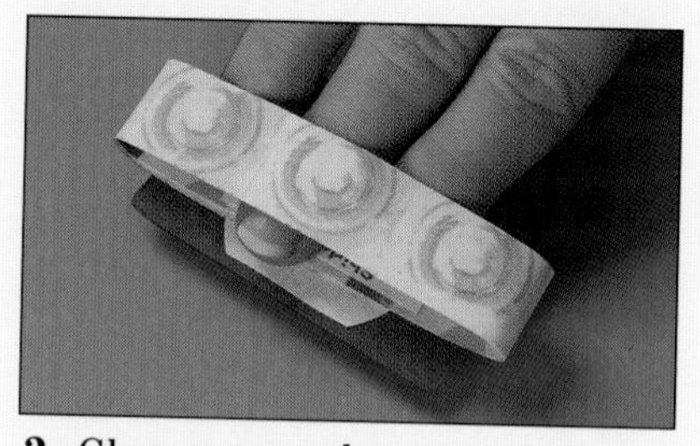

2. Glue paper sleeve to back of camera die-cut.

3. Put tags that are cut out of Tags paper in back pocket.

For an album variation try creating a small accordion album to carry in your purse.

EUROPE 2003 ACCORDION BOOKLET *by Shirley Rufener*

MATERIALS: *Design Originals* Legacy Collage Papers (#0553 Map, #0555 Tags) • *Xyron* machine with permanent adhesive • *Sizzix* die-cutter (film strip & camera dies) • *K & S Metals* 36-gauge Copper tooling foil • Large glass nugget • *Aleene's* Paper Glaze • Fibers

INSTRUCTIONS: Cover two 3" heavy matboard squares with Tags paper to use for the booklet covers. • Cut Maps paper into four 2$^{3}/_{4}$" x 12" strips. • Secure two sets of strips end-to-end. • Roll one through a Xyron machine and secure wrong sides together for page strength. • Fold into a 2$^{3}/_{4}$" accordion. • Secure first page inside album cover and last page inside back cover. • Add photos to both sides with journaling framed in a filmstrip die-cut. • Decorate the cover with a $^{5}/_{8}$" wide paper slip-on tab. • Embellish with an embossed Copper foil camera die-cut with a photo backed glass nugget glued with Paper Glaze. • Add fibers to camera loop.

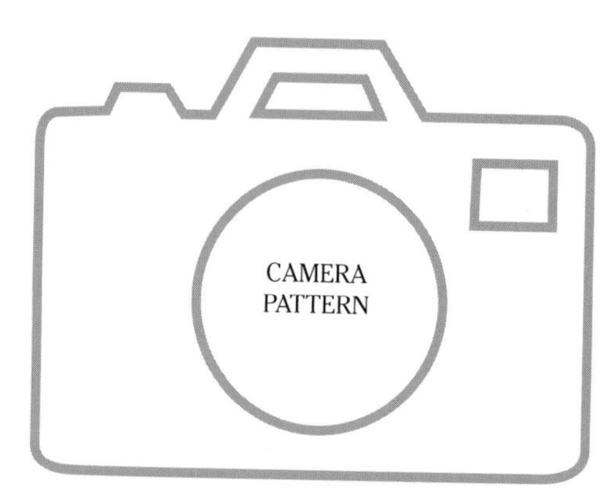

Terrific Tips

• Try making a vacation memory frame using little photos or reduced color copies, secured to larger nuggets.

• Add a printed title and memorabilia from your travels, such as paper umbrellas or inexpensive flower jewelry.

• Surround your treasures with a decoupaged collage frame using *Legacy Collage* Map paper and color coordinating sections of other *Legacy Collage* prints.

MAUI FRAMED MEMORY

by Shirley Rufener

MATERIALS: *Design Originals* Legacy Collage Papers (#0530 Mom's Sewing Box, #0538 Peter's Dreams, #0553 Map, #0554 Diamonds) • 2 large & 4 small glass nuggets • *Aleene's* Instant Decoupage • Paper umbrella • Clay flower earring

Highlight detail areas of photos to magnify the images.

Highlight an entire word by placing a nugget over each letter.

Lettering is always such an important part of any page or project. Think outside the box to create unusual and unique titles for your pages. Eyelets, game pieces, stencils, and even found objects can be used for the most captivating captions. Let your creativity "spell" it out for you.

Combine found objects for clever titles:
Typewriter keys, metal letters, game tiles, metal tiles, stencil letters, nails, hardware and metal discs.

A TRIP TO THE CITY *by Tim Holtz*

MATERIALS: *Design Originals* Legacy Collage Papers (#0549 Shorthand, #0554 Diamonds) • *Petersen Arne* vellum • *Ranger* archival inks (Coffee, Jet Black) • *Ranger* Glossy Accents • *Making Memories* eyelets & letters • *Artistic Wire* 28-gauge Copper wire • *Crafter's Pick* Memory Mount & The Ultimate! • *US ArtQuest* mica • *Rollabind* discs • *River City Rubber Works* Vintage Alphabet rubber stamps • Mini brads • Letter stencils • Wooden letter tiles • Found objects

INSTRUCTIONS: Cut photos to size for page. • Tear edges of Shorthand paper for mats. • Wrinkle paper and distress with Coffee ink using direct to paper technique. • Glue photos to mats with Memory Mount and add 3 eyelets in each corner. • Thread with Copper wire and wrap around approximately 5 times. • Print text on vellum. • Glue text and photos to Diamonds background paper using Memory Mount. • Using The Ultimate!, glue mica tiles and title to top of page. • Create title using metal letters, wood games pieces, stencils, found objects, and faux typewriter keys.

SPRING BREAK

by Tim Holtz

MATERIALS: *Design Originals* Legacy Collage Papers (#0540 Skates, #0545 Ledger, #0550 TeaDye Script, #0484 Blue linen) • *Petersen Arne* vellum • *Crafter's Pick* Memory Mount & The Ultimate! • *Ranger* Glossy Accents • *Ranger* Jet Black Archival Ink • *Making Memories* snaps, brads & letters • *River City Rubber Works* Vintage Alphabet rubber stamps • *Rollabind* disc • Wooden game pieces • Plastic letters • Domino

INSTRUCTIONS: Cut photos to size for page. • For photo mats cut Blue linen paper and tear strip of Skates paper for center. • Secure strip to mat using snaps. • Tear corner piece of TeaDye Script paper and glue to Ledger paper with Memory Mount. • Glue photos to mats and then to page with Memory Mount. • Print text on vellum and secure to page with brads. • Cut strip of vellum and secure to page with snaps. • Create title with metal letters, wood games pieces, a domino, plastic letters, and faux typewriter keys. • With The Ultimate!, glue title to page.

Combine found objects for clever titles: Typewriter keys, metal letters, game tiles, metal tiles, stencil letters, nails, hardware and metal discs, buttons, dominoes and more.

Creative Lettering Ideas for Faux Typewriter Keys

Genuine old typewriter keys are hard to find... create your own dimensional keys with plastic discs.

1. Stamp typewriter key stamp on cardstock using permanent Jet Black Archival Ink or use alphabet stickers.

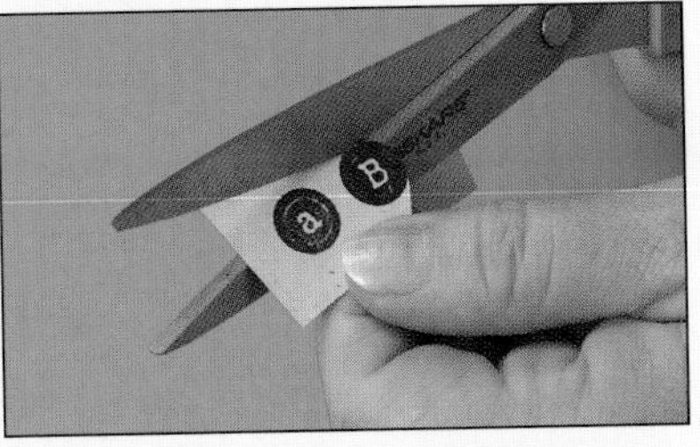

2. Punch out or cut out letter to fit size of Rollabind disc.

3. Using The Ultimate!, glue to inside of disc.

4. Fill inside of disc with Glossy Accents. Let dry.

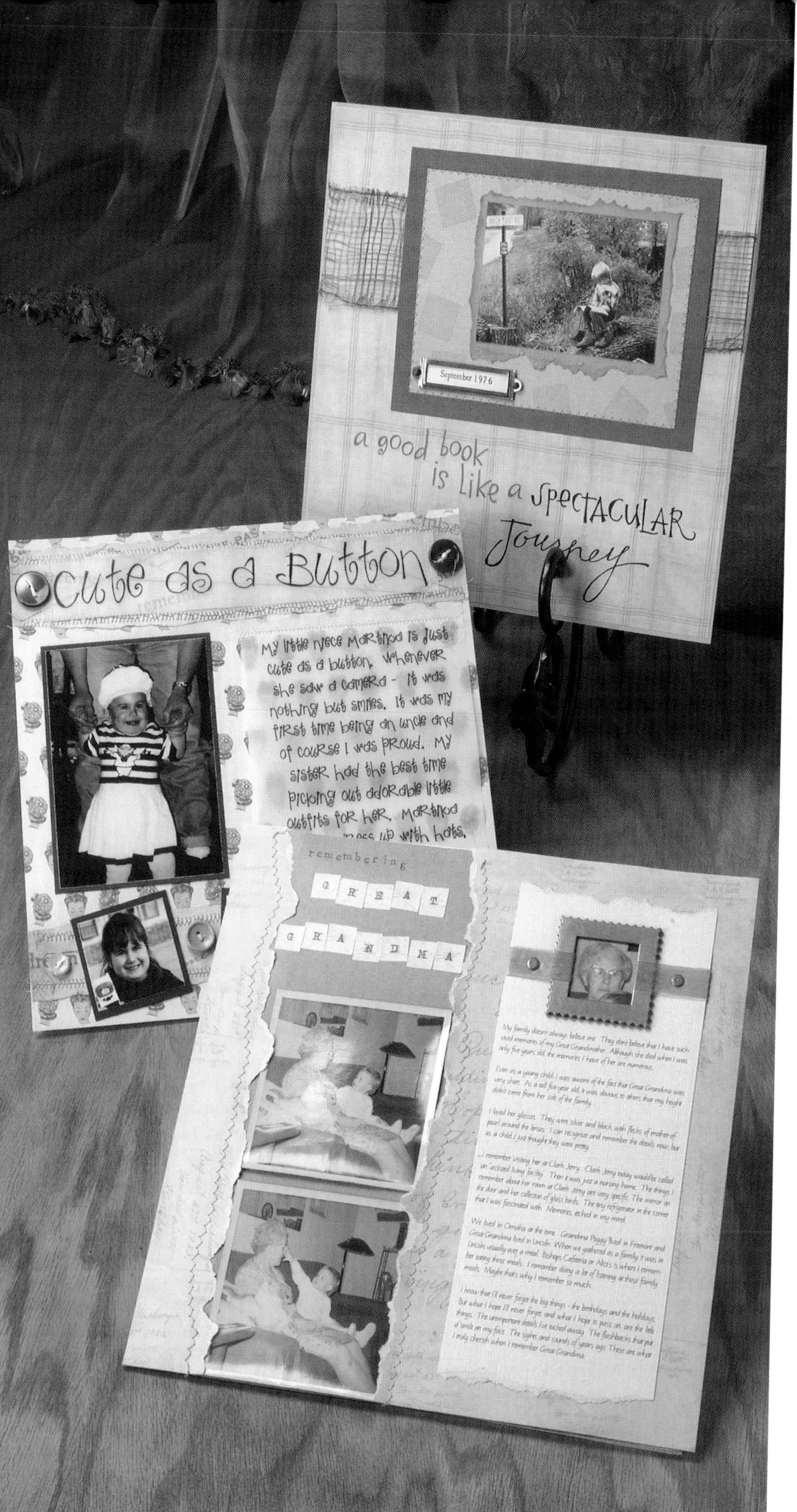

JOURNEY *by Susan Keuter*

MATERIALS: *Design Originals* Legacy Collage Paper (#0539 Plaid Hanky, #0490 Coffee linen) • *Bazzill* cardstock (Light Orange, Pale Blue, Ivory) • *Magic Scraps* Copper Coastal netting • *Colorbök* David Walker letter stickers • *Making Memories* (Simply Stated rub on words, date stamp) • *Two Peas in a Bucket* book plate • Brads • Sewing machine • Light Blue thread

INSTRUCTIONS: Stretch netting across Plaid Hanky paper, fold ends to back and secure. • Mat Plaid Hanky on Pale Blue cardstock. • Stick title to bottom third of page. • Mat photo on torn Light Orange cardstock. • Cut Pale Blue cardstock and Coffee linen paper. • With a zig-zag stitch, sew Pale Blue cardstock to Coffee linen paper together. • Stamp date on Ivory and attach to bookplate. • Attach with bookplate brads. • Add to page with adhesive.

CUTE AS A BUTTON

by Tim Holtz

MATERIALS: *Design Originals* Legacy Collage Papers (#0531 Ladies with Hats, #0551 Legacy Words) • *Petersen Arne* vellum & cardstock • *Ranger* archival ink (Coffee, Mustard) • *Crafter's Pick* Memory Mount & The Ultimate! • *Judikins* Color Duster • Buttons

INSTRUCTIONS: Tear strips of Legacy Words paper for top and bottom of page. • Sew strips to Ladies with Hats background paper. • Distress sewn strips with inks using a Color Duster. • Print title and text on vellum and sew to page to secure. • Mount photos on cardstock and glue to page using Memory Mount. • Using The Ultimate!, glue buttons to page .

REMEMBERING

by Susan Keuter

MATERIALS: *Design Originals* Legacy Collage Papers (#0535 Ruth's Letter) • *Bazzill* cardstock (Cream, Pink) • *Hero Arts* Printer's Lowercase letter stamps • *EK Success* Nostalgiques by Rebecca Sower letter stickers • *Making Memories* (pewter frame, snaps) • *May Arts* sheer Pink ribbon • *Craf-T* chalk • Removable adhesive • Sewing machine • Pale Pink thread

INSTRUCTIONS: Mount collage paper to Pink cardstock with removable adhesive. • Near the center of the paper, lift one edge of collage paper and tear toward yourself. • Tear another edge, tearing toward yourself, and to the left of the first tear, removing about a 4" strip. • Chalk edges with Light Pink. • With a zig-zag stitch, sew collage paper to Pink cardstock ½" from torn edges. • Adhere 2 photos between torn edges. • Attach title letters above photos. • Print journaling on Cream cardstock, tear top and bottom edges. • Trim a photo to fit in frame. • Wrap ribbon around both edges of frame, insert photo and secure to back of cardstock. • Attach to page with adhesive, insert brads through the ribbon.

DRESS UP *by Tim Holtz*

MATERIALS: *Design Originals* Legacy Collage Papers (#0530 Mom's Sewing Box, #0533 Dress Patterns) • *American Tag* small tags • *Ranger* Espresso Adirondack marker • *Ranger* archival inks (Coffee, Sepia) • *Wordsworth* Lettering stencil • *Crafter's Pick* Memory Mount & The Ultimate! • *Judikins* Color Duster • *Petersen Arne* vellum • Wood ruler • Snaps • Buttons • Netting • Pins • Jute Twine • Sewing Machine

INSTRUCTIONS: Cut scrap of netting and sew onto Mom's Sewing Box background paper. • Sew Dress Patterns paper for photo mats and tear edges of mats. • Cut opening for photo with paper trimmer or craft knife. • Glue photos to mats with Memory Mount. • Embellish corners with metal snaps, and mat with pins. • Glue mats to page with Memory Mount. • For title, wrinkle tags and distress with ink using Color Duster. • Using stencil, add a letter to each tag and color with Espresso marker. • Tie to wood ruler with jute and secure ruler with The Ultimate! adhesive. • Print text on vellum and secure to page with pins. • Embellish with buttons using The Ultimate! adhesive.

Add texture by stitching on scrapbook pages.

Stitching on Paper

The technique of stitched pages adds texture and a vintage look to these wonderful printed papers. Add fabric remnants, buttons, snaps, pins, and more. Antique your stitches with ink to create the look of a page right out of Mom's sewing box.

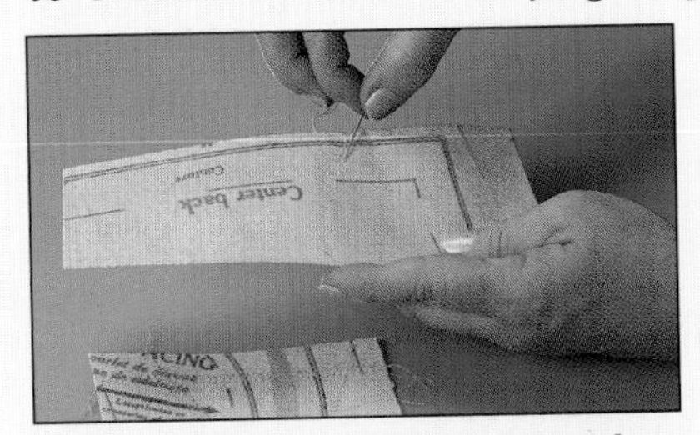

1. Sew paper by hand or with a sewing machine. Sew off the edge.

2. Brush ink over stitches to distress and antique.

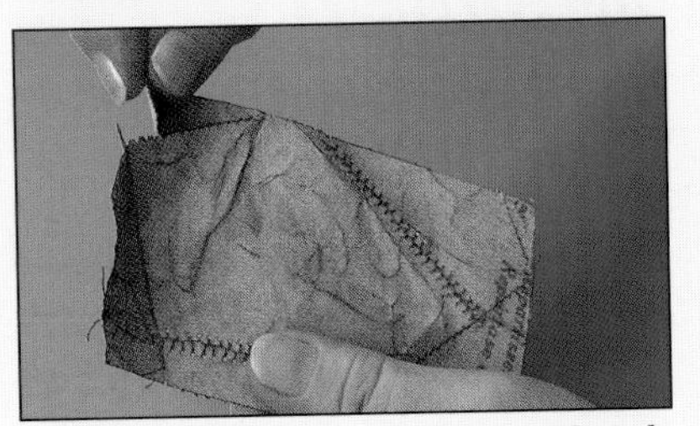

3. Tear or cut edges and ink edges to create a worn look.

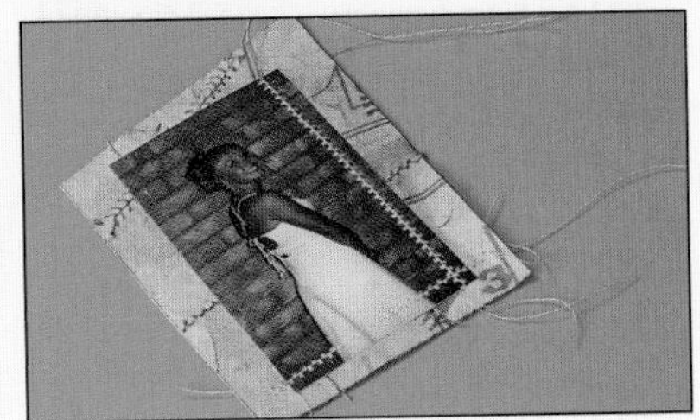

4. Add photos over paper or sew directly onto page.

Bottle Cap Frames - Glue photo into a bottle cap. Use pliers to bend the edges of the bottle cap to the inside to form a frame.

FAMILY HEARTS *by Delores Frantz*

MATERIALS: *Design Originals* Legacy Collage Papers (#0526 Two Ladies, #0528 Watches, 2 of #0540 Skates, 3 of #0478 Green linen, 3 of #0479 Green stripe, 2 of #0480 Green floral) • Vellum • Journaling & cursive computer fonts • *ColorBox* Cat's Eye Chestnut Roan chalking ink • 60" of Burgundy pearl cotton floss • 28 Pink eyelets • Eyelet setter • 8 Bottle caps • Scallop scissors • Circle punches (1/16", 1/8", 1") • Hammer

INSTRUCTIONS: Glue 2 sets of floral and stripe papers together, back to back. • Cut 2 large half hearts. • Glue Watches and Green stripe papers together, back to back. • Cut 2 medium half hearts. • Age the edges of the hearts. • Punch 1/16" holes along the edge of large heart halves. • Lace floss or fibers through the holes. • Punch 1/8" holes along the edge of medium heart halves. • Set eyelets in holes. • Prepare background pages. • Glue edges of large, medium and small hearts to the spine of each album page. • Punch a 1" circle of a face from a photo. • Glue photo into a bottle cap. • Use pliers to bend the edges of the bottle cap to the inside to form a frame. • Crimp the edges flat.

Layering... Creating & Attaching Pages

This fabulous page has several layers... each one embellished and packed with family memories. Preserving joyful memories of family activities - birthday parties, new babies, achievements in school, holidays and reunions adds to the importance of family.

1. Glue 2 sets of Floral and Stripe papers together, back to back. Cut 2 large hearts.

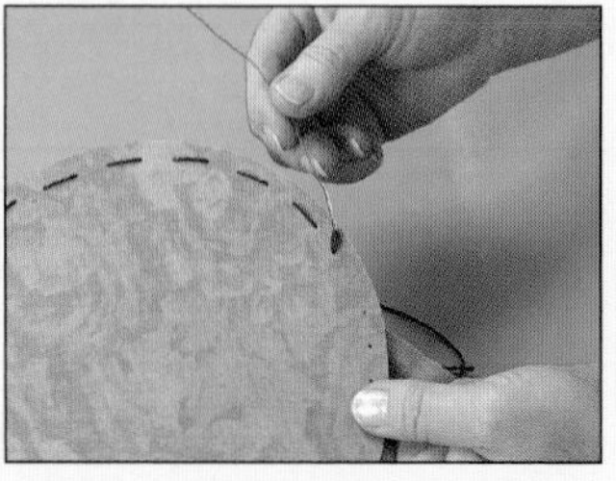

2. Punch 1/16" holes along the edge of large hearts. Lace floss or fibers through the holes.

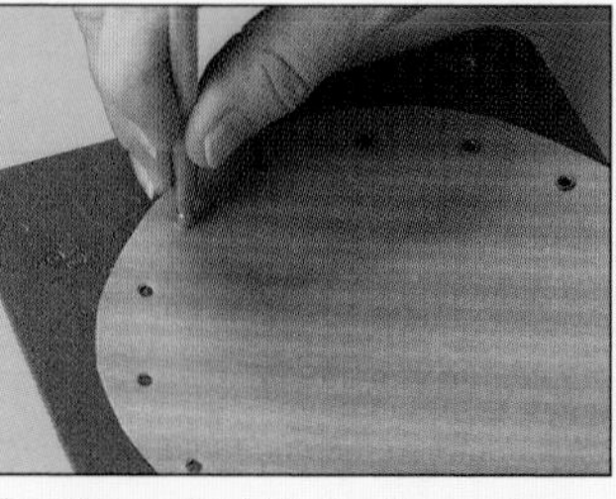

3. Punch 1/8" holes along the edge of medium hearts. Set eyelets in holes.

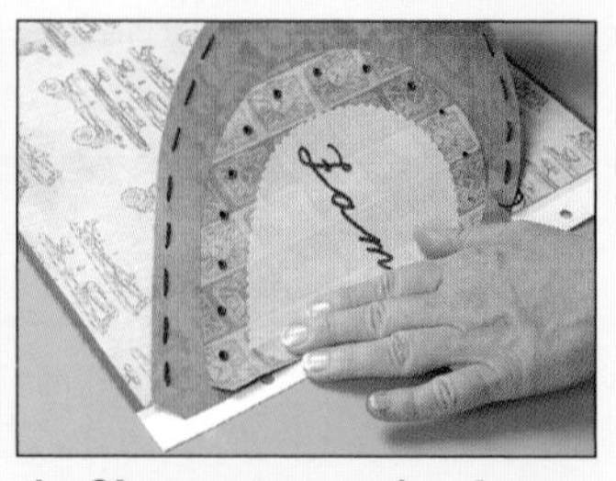

4. Glue spines of a large, medium and small heart to the spine of each album page.

Bottle cap frames.

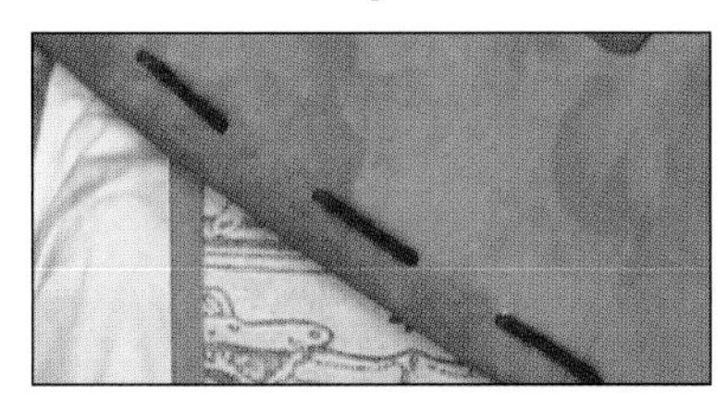

Stitching along the edge.

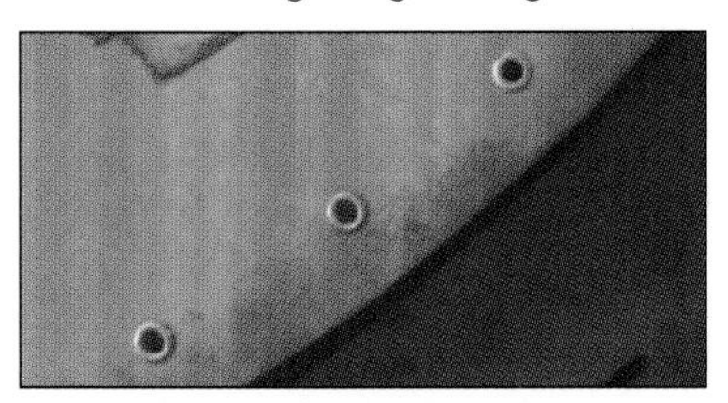

Eyelets along the edge.

Cut out images of clock faces.

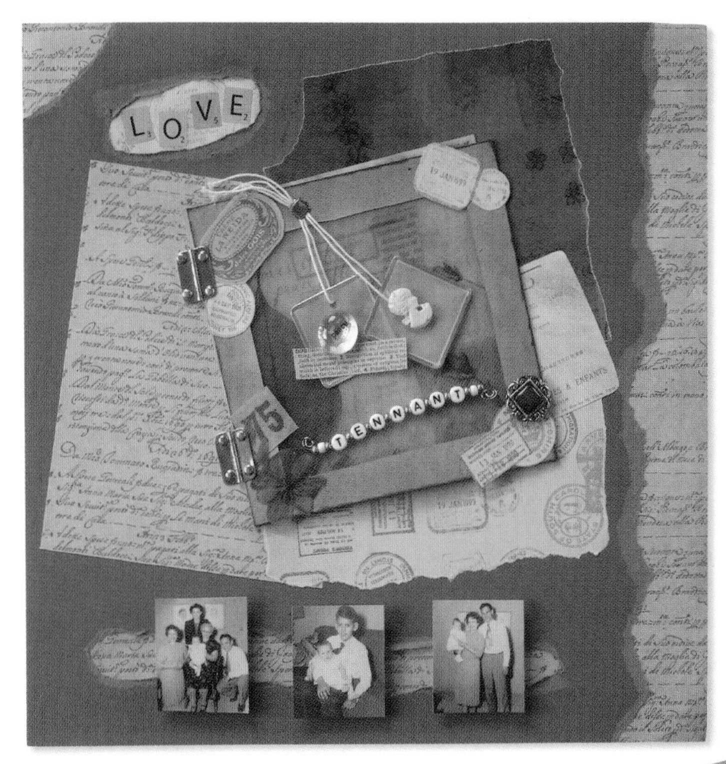

'LOVE' with OPEN BOOKLET *by Katrina Hogan*

MATERIALS: *Design Originals* Legacy Collage Papers (#0529 Le Jardin, #0538 Peter's Dreams, #0547 Dictionary, #0548 Passport, #0550 TeaDye Script)• Cardstock (Olive, Ecru) • *Autumn Leaves* printed vellum • *PSX* letter stickers • *Jesse James* buttons • *Making Memories* tags & letter tiles • *Jest Charming* eyelet letters • *Stop N Crop* hinges • *ColorBox* Cat's Eye chalking ink • Clear glass nugget • 26-gauge Gold wire • Pop dots

INSTRUCTIONS: Layer cardstock over printed paper. • Tear upper left-hand corner and approximately 1" of the right side of cardstock. • Use a water pen to draw an oval in cardstock and tear on the water line. • Adhere cardstock to patterned paper. • Layer several different patterned papers in the center of the cardstock.

To create a book, cut two squares approximately 5 1/2" x 5 1/2". • Cut out 4" x 4" opening in center. • Layer a piece of patterned vellum between the two frames, glue together. • Add two hinges, mount on 5 1/2" x 5 1/2" cardstock on page. • Embellish page, aging papers as desired.

GET WELL CARD and ENVELOPE

by Delores Frantz

MATERIALS: *Design Originals* Legacy Collage Papers (#0528 Watches, #0534 Ruth's Violets, #0539 Plaid Hanky, #0486 Blue floral, #0509 Florals cut) • Ivory cardstock • Vellum • Cardboard letter tiles • *ColorBox* Cat's Eye Chestnut Roan chalking ink • 10 Gold eyelets • Eyelet setter • Gold hand charm • 24" Fiber

INSTRUCTIONS: Cut floral paper 5 1/2" x 8 1/2", fold to make card. • Adhere 4" x 5 1/4" Watches paper to card front. • Tear Ruth's Violets figures, attach to Watches. • Add a floral cut to edge of figures. • Age edges of 3 3/4" x 5" vellum; attach to card front. • Mat 'Get Well' letter tiles, place on vellum. • Tear a strip of floral paper the height of card. • Attach to folded edge with eyelets. • Lace fiber through eyelets, attaching hand charm before making a bow.

For envelope adhere Watches paper to Plaid Hanky paper, back to back. • Fold into envelope. • Apply Floral cuts and watches to outside of envelope.

ANDY AND TESS *by Delores Frantz*

MATERIALS: *Design Originals* Legacy Collage Papers (#0534 Ruth's Violets, #0538 Peter's Dreams, #0541 Report Card, #0547 Dictionary, (#0490 Coffee linen, #0491 Coffee stripe) • *Design Originals* Legacy Cut (#0507 Shoe) • White vellum • *ColorBox* Cat's Eye Chestnut Roan chalking ink • 10 Large square metal eyelets • *Making Memories* Square metal letter tiles • Wooden game letter tiles • Ruler

INSTRUCTIONS: Glue $11^1/_2$" square of Dictionary paper to a full sheet of Coffee linen paper. • Tear images and age the edges with Roan chalk. • Arrange images and photo on the page leaving $2^1/_2$" free on the left side of page. • Press a ruler on Coffee Stripe paper and tear a $2^1/_2$" strip. • Cut 11" square of vellum. • Place vellum and strip on page. • Attach with eyelets. • Thread fiber through eyelets and tie a bow.

Vellum Pages

Vellum is such a wonderful paper... its translucent quality enables you to create fabulous cards and scrapbook pages. The unique translucent quality allows combination with photos, vintage images, titles, journaling and more.

1. Press a ruler on Coffee stripe paper and tear a $2^1/_2$" strip.

2. Attach strip with eyelets. Thread fiber through eyelets and tie a bow.

Add an aged strip of vellum on the border.

LOVING ALL THINGS EQUINE

by Carol Wingert

MATERIALS: *Design Originals* Legacy Collage Paper (#0547 Dictionary) • Cardstock (Ecru, Light Brown) • *Manto Fev* 2" x 2" silver slide mount and letter tile • *Ellison* die-cuts (number 2 and tag) • *Savage* Glassine envelope • *Anima Designs* Aluminum tags • *Coffee Break Design* eyelets • *Missing Link Stamp Co.* Alphabet rubber stamps • *ColorBox* Ancient Page stamping ink • *Ranger* Adirondack aging ink • *7 gypsies* waxed linen • 26-gauge Silver wire • *Amaco* Silver wire mesh

INSTRUCTIONS: Using Dictionary paper as background, adhere 1$^1/_2$" wide torn strip of Brown cardstock to right center. • Age papers with aging ink. • To create the letter slide mount, cut a piece of cardstock to fit into slide mount. • Layer a piece of wire mesh over the cardstock. • Place letter tile over the wire and determine position of eyelets. • Set eyelets. • Secure letter tile with thin wire. • Insert title stamped on Ecru cardstock into glassine envelope and slide through the slide mount. • Computer generate top title and add Aluminum tags to each end. • Adhere titles, photo and computer generated definition. • Add tag with '2' on it. • Hand-stitch across Brown strip with waxed linen. Tie each stitch in a knot to secure.

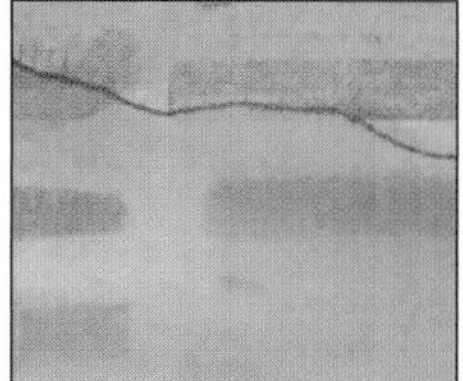

Add a torn and aged vellum overlay on page.

Add a second layer of torn vellum for a border.

PROUD GRANDPA *by Tim Holtz*

MATERIALS: *Design Originals* Legacy Collage Papers (#0542 Farm House, #0543 Brushes, #0494 Brown stripe) • *Petersen Arne* vellum & kraft cardstock • *Ranger* Coffee Archival ink • *Judikins* Color Duster • *Crafter's Pick* Memory Mount & The Ultimate! • *Making Memories* metal-rimmed tags

INSTRUCTIONS: Use Farm House paper for background. • Lay vellum over page and create windows. • Cut photos to size for page. • Cut mats for photos with Brushes and Brown stripe papers. • Glue photos to mats and mats to page with Memory Mount. • Print title on vellum and glue to page with Memory Mount. • Print photo captions on kraft cardstock, tear and distress with Coffee ink. • Tear out inside of metal rimmed tags and glue frame to page using The Ultimate! adhesive. • Glue captions over frame at angle using Memory Mount.

Vellum Overlays

The use of vellum paper creates a soft, diffused look to your pages. By creating windows in the vellum, you can reveal the favorite parts of your background paper and add dimension to your pages. Who knows what you might find when you peek through the soft windows of time.

1. Select background paper, lay vellum over the top. Using a pencil lightly draw around areas you would like revealed as windows.

2. Tear or cut out area using the pencil lines as your guide.

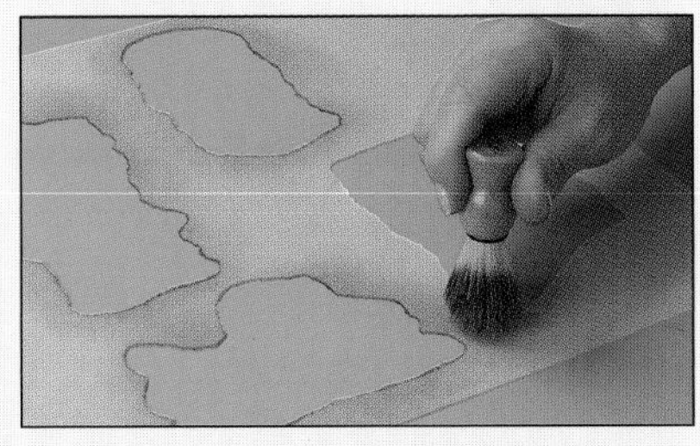

3. Using Color Duster, ink edges of windows to create contrast.

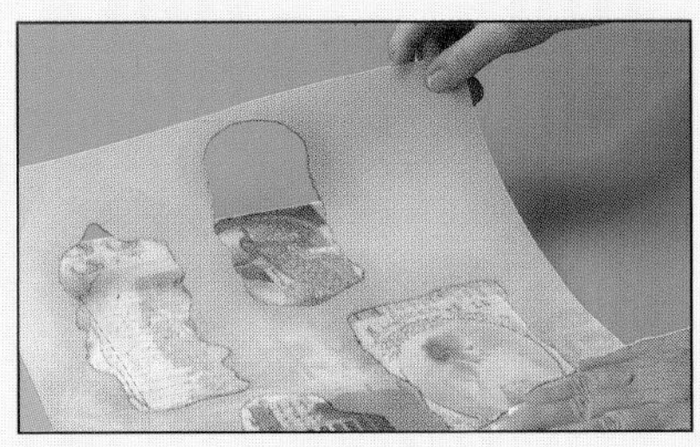

4. Glue vellum over background paper, lining up windows to the areas you want to reveal.

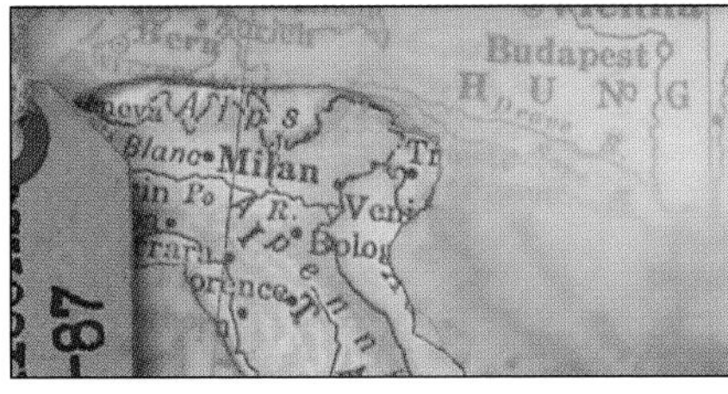

Tear and age sections of the vellum.

Add tag to journal special events.

Use Passport paper to tell the story.

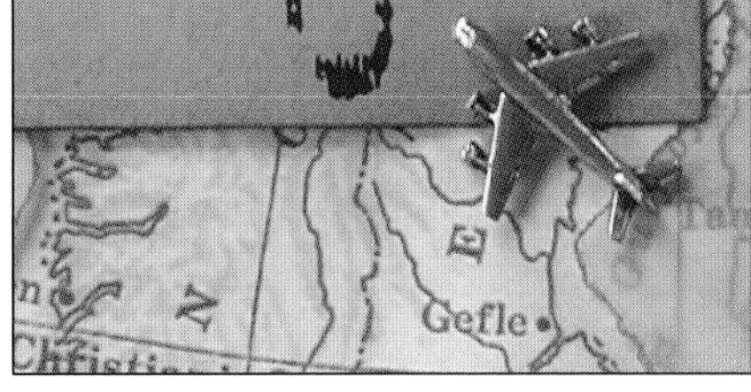

Use Map paper as the background.

TAKE FLIGHT *by Tim Holtz*

MATERIALS: *Design Originals* Legacy Collage Papers (#0548 Passport, #0553 Map, #0493 Brown linen) • *Petersen Arne* vellum & kraft cardstock • *Ranger* Sepia Archival ink • *Making Memories* eyelets • *Emagination Crafts* tag punch • *Crafter's Pick* Memory Mount & The Ultimate! • *Judikins* Color Duster • Airplane charm • Jute twine

INSTRUCTIONS: Using Map paper for background, lay vellum over page and create windows to highlight countries. • Glue to Map paper with Memory Mount. • Cut photos to size for page. • Cut mats for photos with Brown linen paper. • Glue mats to photos with Memory Mount. • Add 2 eyelets per corner and tie corners with jute. • Tear strip of Passport paper and distress with Sepia ink using a Color Duster. • Glue torn strip of Passport paper and photos to vellum with Memory Mount. • Print title and tag info on kraft cardstock. • Punch tag info using tag punch. • Age tag with Sepia ink. • Tie tags to photos with jute. • Glue title and secure tags to page with Memory Mount. • Glue charm to page using The Ultimate! adhesive.

MEN ARE LIKE FINE WINE

by Mary Kaye Seckler

MATERIALS: *Design Originals* Legacy Collage Papers (#0526 Two Ladies, #0552 Travels) • $5^{1}/_{2}$" square White card • White square doily • *Ranger Adirondack* Cranberry ink pad • *ColorBox* Chestnut Cat's Eye chalking ink • *Imagine* 'Men are like fine wine' rubber stamp • Double-stick mounting tape

INSTRUCTIONS: Stipple card front with Cranberry ink. • Tear lady image out of Travels paper, edge with Cranberry ink and adhere to card with double-stick mounting tape. • Color outer part of doily with Cranberry ink. • Stamp 'Men are like..' with Cranberry ink in doily center. • Fold the four sides over to make a little packet. • Line inside of card with Two Ladies paper. • Adhere doily packet to inside of card with craft glue.

Unfold all four sides of the paper doily to reveal a lovely poem or note.

Create a Beautiful Card with a Doily that Unfolds to Reveal a Poem!

Open the card to reveal the folded paper doily.

Decorate the outside of the card with papers.

Making Collage Buttons

Making your own embellishments with clear acrylic buttons and papers is easy.

1. Select text from a Dictionary paper. Stipple with fluid chalk or ink.

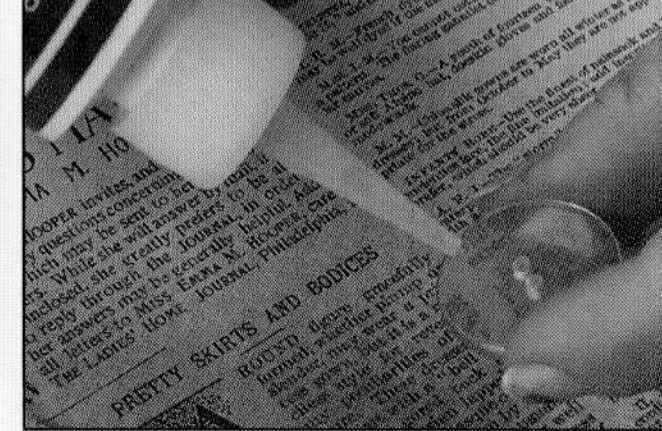

2. Apply Diamond Glaze to one side of a clear acrylic button. Press button onto text paper, let dry.

3. Trim around the button.

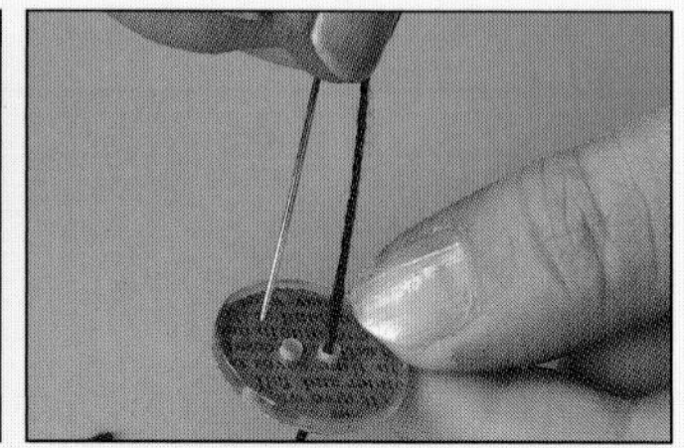

4. Attach to page with wire. Twist wire on the back of page. Cover wire with tape.

LUCKY SPEISTY

by Mary Kaye Seckler

MATERIALS: *Design Originals* Legacy Collage Papers (#0547 Dictionary, #0551 Legacy Words) • Cardstock (Blue, Tan) • *Amscan* White rectangle doily • *ColorBox* Cat's Eye chalking ink (Colonial Blue, Chestnut) • *Marvy* #18 Brown ink pad • *Ranger* Adirondack Caramel ink pad • *Missing Link* alphabet rubber stamps • *On the Surface* antique buttons, Copper metallic thread • Clear acrylic buttons • Gold eyelets • *Stamp Asylum* plain brass charms • 3/8" metal letters - available at any hardware store • Hammer • Anvil • Bench block • Black acrylic paint • *Making Memories* metal glue • *Judikins* Diamond Glaze • Brown thread • Alligator clips • Torch • Tape

INSTRUCTIONS: Age edges of Legacy Words paper with Chestnut ink. • Set gold eyelets in top sides of page 1" in and 1 1/2" down. • Stamp 'Lucky' on Blue cardstock; tear out and age edges with Colonial Blue and Chestnut inks. • With hammer and anvil, impress title letters into charms; highlight with Black acrylic paint. • Holding charm with alligator clips, briefly age with a torch. Overheating will result in a dusty grey color. • String charms on fiber; space across page and glue. • Stipple doily with Caramel ink and edge with Chestnut ink. • Mat photo; adhere to doily and doily to page. • Mat journaling and adhere to page. • Adhere aged Dictionary text to clear acrylic buttons with Diamond Glaze. • Trim copy around button and attach to page with thread.

Making Lace Frames with Doilies

Age a doily for a vintage look.

1. Tint doily and edge with Cat's Eye fluid chalk or ink.

2. Edge blue photo mat with fluid chalk or ink.

3. Adhere mat to the aged paper doily.

Aging Metal Charms with Heat

Antique impressed letters with acrylic paint. If desired, alter the metal color with a torch.

1. Impress title into plain brass charms with metal letters.

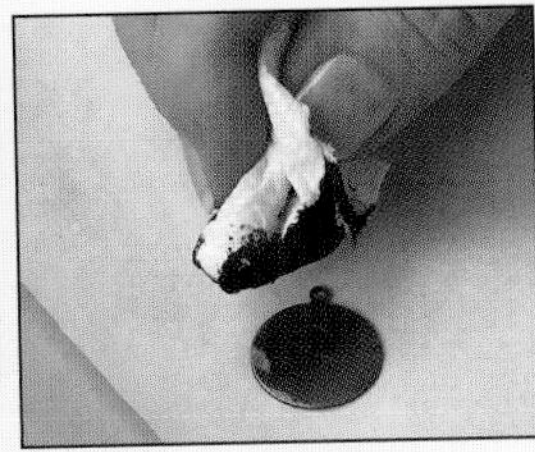

2. Highlight letters by rubbing Black acrylic paint into them.

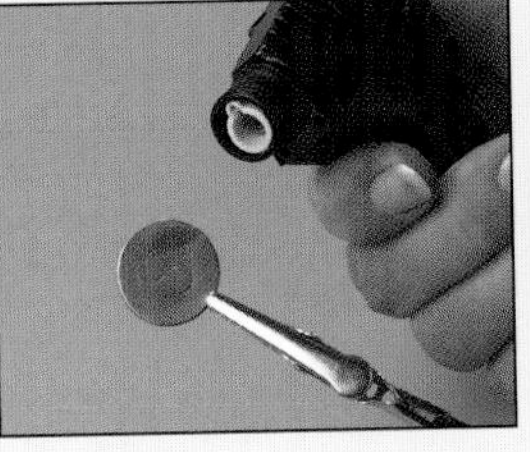

3. Hold charm with an alligator clip and briefly fire with a torch.

4. Thread the charms on fiber. Affix ends to the back of the page with tape.

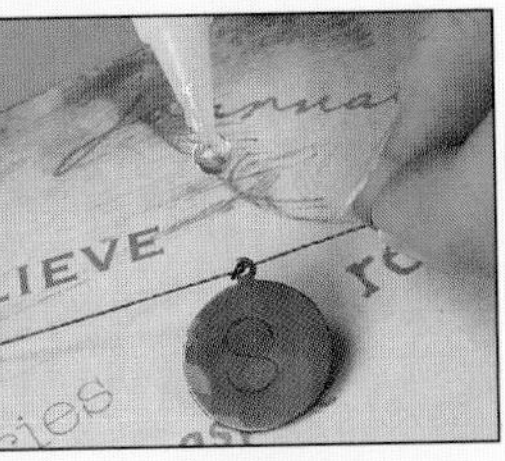

5. Space the charms across the page and affix with glue.

Making the Title for 'Sarah'

1. Trace letters onto cardstock and cut out.

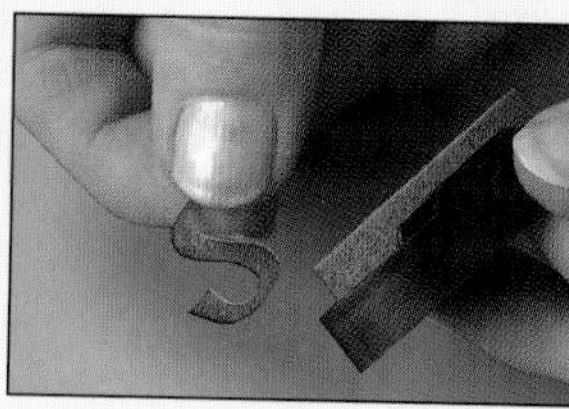
2. Edge letters with fluid chalk or ink.

3. Adhere letters to page.

UNITED IN PURPOSE *by Carol Wingert*

MATERIALS: *Design Originals* Legacy Collage Papers (#0543 Brushes, #0550 TeaDye Script, #0493 Brown linen) • *Golden* Matte and Gel Medium • Canvas cloth • *Artchix Studio* optical lens • *7 gypsies* Walnut Ink and Spiral • *Coffee Break Design* eyelets • Rubber stamps (*Hero Arts* Alphabet; *Paper Inspirations* Vine) • *Ranger* Adirondack aging and stamping ink • *Making Memories* Tiny Brad • Paint brush • Pinking shears • Hemp • Brayer • Teaspoon

INSTRUCTIONS: To create an acrylic medium transfer onto canvas, color copy photo onto lightweight paper. • Cut a piece of canvas cloth about 1" larger than photo on all four sides. • Apply Golden matte medium to canvas with a brush. • Using your fingers, apply Golden gel medium over the matte medium, applying enough so that it doesn't dry quickly. • Lay photo, copy side down into the gel medium. Use a brayer to remove any air pockets or wrinkles. • Using the underside of a teaspoon, burnish the paper to the canvas. It is important that the entire surface be consistently burnished so that there aren't patches where the image did not transfer. • Allow to dry overnight. • To remove the paper the next day, lay canvas and paper into a baking dish of water. • As the paper softens, gently rub it off with fingertips (Caution: heavy rubbing may pull the transfer off the canvas). • When the paper is removed, lightly apply walnut ink to any light or untransferred areas, as well as to the edges of the image area. • Allow to dry. • When dry, paint on a protective coat of matte medium. • Adhere torn TeaDye Script paper to the bottom two-thirds of your layout page. • Create a top fold-over piece with torn Brown linen and Brushes paper. Adhere and machine stitch. • Add eyelets and tie with hemp between eyelets. • When canvas image transfer is dry, cut edges with pinking shears and machine stitch to torn cardstock. • Adhere to layout. • Add aged title, aged stamped envelope and optical lens with computer generated journaling. • Add embellishments.

Age Papers

1. Tint paper with glazes.

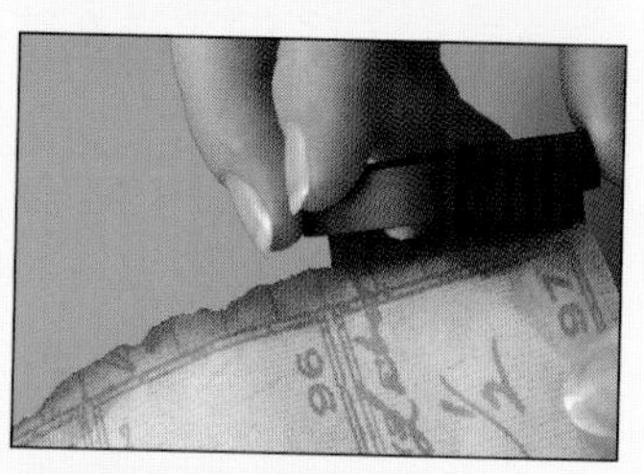
2. Age edges with fluid chalks or inks.

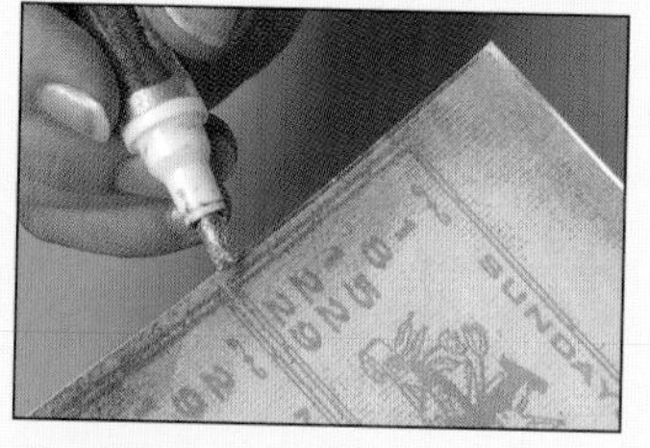
3. Edge along the sides with a metallic gold pen.

Stitching

1. Adhere strip to page.

2. Pierce holes with awl.

3. Stitch with gold thread.

SIMPLY SARAH *by Mary Kaye Seckler*

MATERIALS: *Design Originals* Legacy Collage Papers (#0545 Ledger, #0550 TeaDye Script) • Golden Brown cardstock • *PSX* Gold mulberry paper • *Golden* glazes (Burnt Umber, Yellow Ochre) • Sea sponge • Rubber stamps (*Stampers Anonymous* crackle cube; *Hero Arts* tiny carnival letters) • Inks (*Marvy* #18 Brown; *ColorBox* Cat's Eye Chestnut; *Ranger* Adirondack Caramel) • Seven 2$^{3}/_{14}$" x 1$^{7}/_{8}$" tags • *On the Surface* Gold metallic thread and fibers • *Pagerz* small calligraphy template • *Krylon* Gold leaf pen • *Scrappy's* gold metal corners • *Tombow* Mono Multi glue • *Sailor* Two-in-One glue pen • Awl

INSTRUCTIONS: Sponge glazes around edges of page; let dry. • Stamp crackle cube with Brown ink randomly around edges. • Apply Gold leaf pen around edges. • Tear off left portion of Ledger paper; sponge edges with glazes and let dry. • Stamp crackle cube around left, bottom and top edges. • Edge right side with Chestnut ink. • Edge all four sides with Gold leaf pen. • Adhere strip to TeaDye Script paper. • Pierce holes and hand-sew pockets in strip. • Cut tags from cardstock (3 Yellow and 4 Caramel); edge with Gold leaf pen. • Stamp letters on tags. • Add fibers; slide into pockets. • Trace and cut title letters from cardstock; edge with Chestnut. • Adhere to page with Sailor glue pen. • With a wet brush and ruler, trace outline of mat onto mulberry paper; tear along wet lines. • Tint edges with Caramel; then edge with Gold leaf pen. • Adhere photo to mat, mat to page and Gold metal corners to photo.

Making Tags

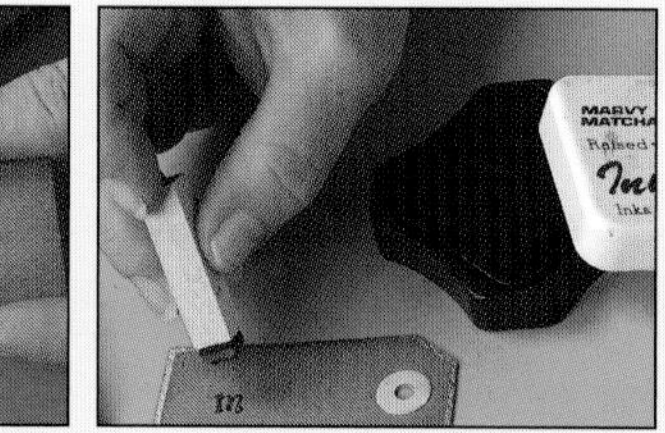

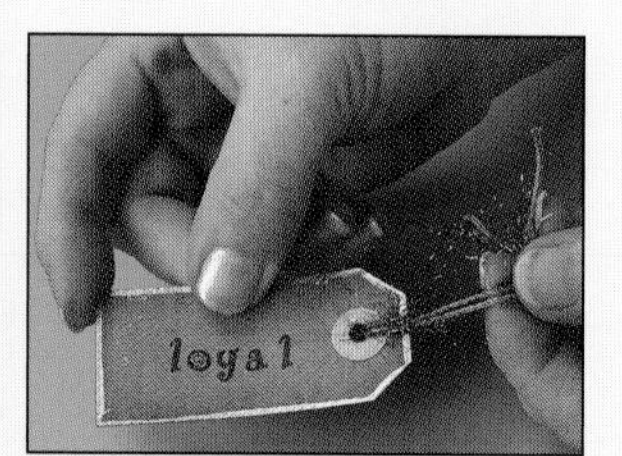

1. Age tags with ink. Edge with Gold leaf pen.

2. Stamp letters on tags.

3. Add fibers to tags.

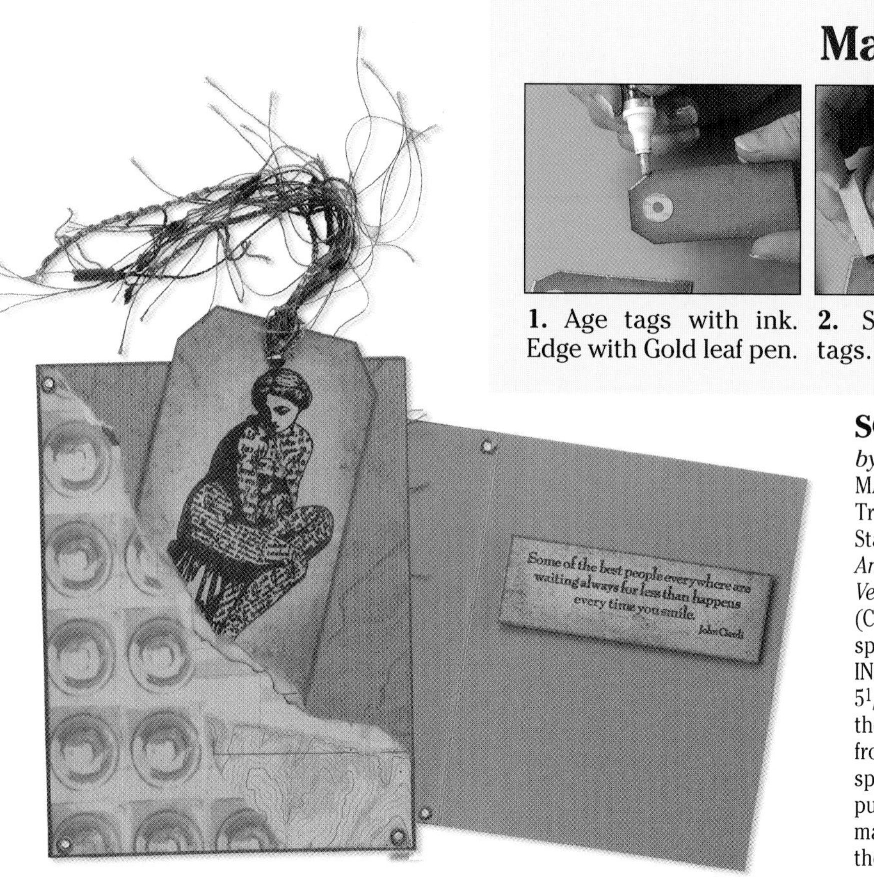

SOME OF THE BEST PEOPLE

by Mary Kaye Seckler

MATERIALS: *Design Originals* Legacy Collage Paper (#0552 Travels) • Cardstock (Celery Green, Cream) • Rubber Stamps (*A Lost Art* 'Some of the best people'; *Stampers Anonymous* #P120 Statue) • Ink pads (*Marvy* #18 Brown; *Versacolor* Green Tea and Bamboo) • *SMI* soft chalk pastels (Celery, Medium Green, Brown) • *Krylon* Workable Fix spray sealer • 3 Light Green eyelets • *On the Surface* fibers

INSTRUCTIONS: Fold Celery Green cardstock into 4 1/4" x 5 1/2" card. • Tear the corner from Travels paper, edge with the Green Tea and Bamboo inks and attach to the card front with eyelets. • Rub chalks onto Cream cardstock; spray with a sealer and let dry. • Stamp statue in brown ink, punch a hole in the top and attach fibers. • Insert the bookmark in the pocket. • Stamp 'Some of the best people' on the inside of the card.

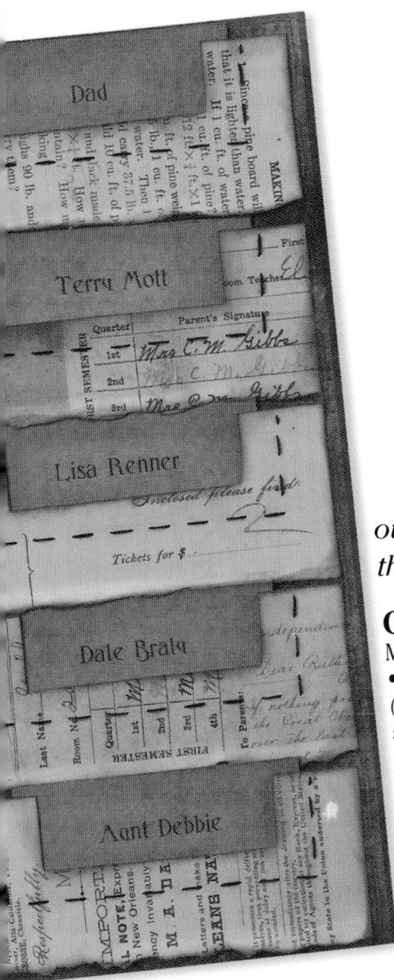

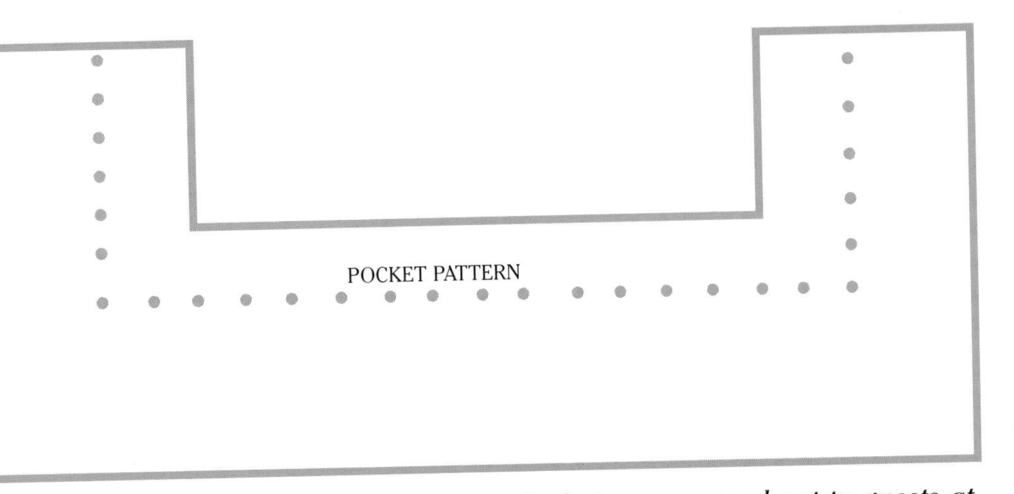

This scrapbook layout was done using cards that were passed out to guests at our daughter's graduation party. The cards asked for each guest's best advice and this is how I preserved their advice.

OUR BEST ADVICE *by Mary Kaye Seckler*

MATERIALS: *Design Originals* Legacy Collage Papers (2 sheets #0528 Watches, 2 sheets #0541 Report Card) • Cardstock (Cream, Burgundy) • Encaustic art iron and waxes (Clear, Red, Gold and Copper) • *SMI* Artist chalk pastels (Bright Orange, Burnt Orange, Terra Cotta) • *Krylon* Workable Fix spray sealer • *Stampers Anonymous* cube alphabet stamps • Ink pads (*Marvy* #18 Brown; *Colorbox* Cat's Eye Chestnut and Merlot) • *Chubby* Monoline Wordsworth lettering template • Burgundy floss • Piece of chipboard • Awl • Foam dots

INSTRUCTIONS: Apply wax to Watches paper with the encaustic iron in the following order: clear first, then colors in random patches around the edges of the papers. • Chalk preprinted cards beginning with light colors and progressing to darker shades; seal with Krylon sealer. • Make a pocket template using the chipboard; pierce holes in the templates to mark the holes for sewing. • Trace each pocket onto Report Card paper, marking the sewing holes with an awl. • Tear the bottom of each pocket rather than cutting and smudge all the edges of the pocket with a Chestnut Cat's Eye. • Sew the pockets on using two strands of burgundy floss. • Insert the advice cards into the pockets. • Mount photo and journaling on cardstock edged with a Merlot Cat's Eye. • Stamp 'Nicole' with brown ink; cut out, edge and mount on foam dots. • Trace title with the lettering stencil; cut out and attach above the journaling block.

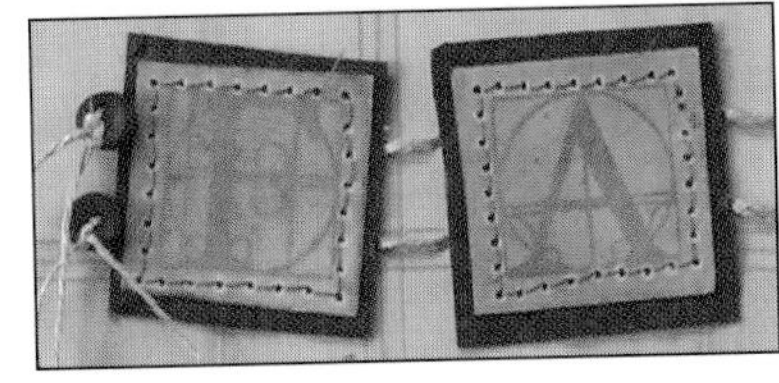

Stitch around each square.

FALL *by Carol Wingert*

MATERIALS: *Design Originals* Legacy Collage Paper (#0539 Plaid Hanky, #0487 Rust linen) • Ecru cardstock • *Memory Lane* Rust leather paper • 2" x 2" slide mount • *Hampton Art Stamps* Codex Alphabet rubber stamps • *ColorBox* Cat's Eye chalking ink • *Golden* acrylic glazes • Natural linen thread • *Hillcreek Designs* buttons • Foam tape

INSTRUCTIONS: Paint slide mount with layers of acrylic glazes. Set aside to dry. • Stamp "FALL" on cardstock with chalk ink, using a codex alphabet. • Age and cut out letter squares. • Mount squares on leather paper and cut into slightly larger squares. • Machine stitch together on all four sides. • Adhere photos to Rust linen paper. • Add a torn and aged strip of Plaid Hanky paper. • Adhere "FALL" letters to aged strip and hand-stitch together with linen thread. • Add mini buttons to the end of each thread and tie in a knot to secure. • Adhere photo to back of slide mount. • Add a piece of torn and aged Plaid Hanky paper behind the mount and adhere to layout with foam tape.

Metal Die-Cut Shapes

1. Apply Xyron permanent adhesive to a similar color of cardstock.

2. Secure foil to cardstock. Die-cut shape, metal side up, on Sizzix.

Antiquing Metal

1. Place metal on scratch paper. Apply ink with dauber.

2. Wipe excess ink immediately with a soft cloth.

Embossing Metal

Use a simple pointed tool to emboss metal.

1. Place metal foil shape on craft foam. Emboss details with a stylus.

2. Puff the back using a rounded wood sculpting tool to give dimension.

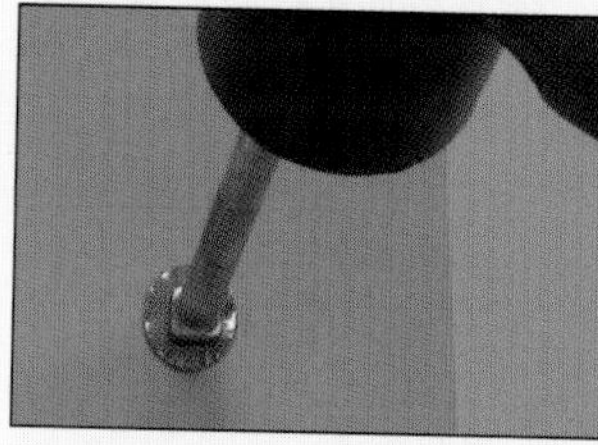

3. With metal foil on craft foam, firmly hit the head of a metal leather stamp with a mallet.

4. Emboss words with a stylus placing the back side of a letter template on the back of metal foil.

Coloring Wire

1. Place wire mesh on scratch paper. Apply a solid layer of StazOn ink with a dauber.

2. Use mesh as a stencil. Two colors of ink create more texture.

Aging Metal

1. Apply a solid coverage of StazOn ink with dauber. Blot ink to variegate color.

Emboss and Shape Thin Metal to Embellish Pages!

PROM NIGHT *by Shirley Rufener*

MATERIALS: *Design Originals* Legacy Collage Papers (2 of #0526 Two Ladies, #0528 Watches) • Cardstock (Cranberry, Deep Gray) • *K & S Metals* 36-gauge Copper tooling foil • 26-gauge Copper wire • *Sizzix* die-cutter (Leaf Stem die) • *EK Success* Paper Shaper Block Upper "O" punch (#PSM15CS) • *Aleene's* Memory Glue • *Tsukineko StazOn* Jet Black ink pad, *Brilliance* Cosmic Copper ink pad • Heavy weight vellum • Metallic Bronze 'E' beads • Flower rhinestones • Mini connected rhinestone chain • *Xyron* 510 machine with permanent adhesive • Mini adhesive foam dots • *Leather Factory* 1/4" alphabet/number leather stamp set • *Fiskars* Metalworks scissors • Double-sided adhesive • 1/16" hole punch • Heat Tool • *Loew-Cornell* Rounded/tapered wooden clay modeling tool • *JudiKins* Color Duster applicator brush • Mallet

INSTRUCTIONS: Double mat photos with Watches paper then torn cardstock. • Secure to Two Ladies background. • Heat foil to intensify color and let cool. • Die-cut two foil leaves and emboss veins. • Punch 4 oval plates at least 1/4" from edge of foil. Set aside. • Using foil openings, cut 4 oval frames 1/8" larger. Create vellum tags. • Place foil under background paper, emboss watch frame with stylus and cut out from foil. Emboss details. • Stamp letters on foil plates. Re-flatten foil with straight end of modeling tool. • Antique leaves, plates and watch frame. • Mount paper to cardstock. • Thread beaded wire through plates (and oval tags) and use foam tape under foil to secure. • Secure watch and leaves with foam dots, and rhinestones with glue. • Tear around ladies face, round label and a watch in remaining sheet of printed paper. • Use duster brush to apply Copper ink to torn edges, and light areas of paper background. • Glue paper designs to page.

LETTER OVAL

WATCH

NUMBER OVAL

BOY'S DREAM *by Shirley Rufener*

MATERIALS: *Design Originals* Legacy Collage Papers (#0532 Red Patterns, #0538 Peter's Dreams) • Black cardstock • *K & S Metals* 36-gauge Copper & Aluminum tooling foil • *Sizzix* die-cutter (Airplane die #38-0126 & Baseball Gear die #38-0289) • *Quickutz* Die-cutter (Venus Alphabet & Shadow Alphabet) • *Tsukineko* Black *StazOn* ink pad • 24 silver 1/8" eyelets • 1/8" eyelet setting tool and hole punch • Brown Twistel cording • *Xyron* machine with permanent adhesive • *Aleene's* Memory Glue • Double-sided adhesive tape • Foam dots

INSTRUCTIONS: Cut off 3/4" strip from left edge of Peter's Dreams paper and add a strip of Red Patterns paper behind so it is 12" wide again. • Mark and punch 2 rows of 12 holes 1" apart on paper, set eyelets. • Weave "X" pattern with twistel. Tape ends to back side. • Secure double-matted photo to page with tape. • Die-cut Aluminum shapes, emboss details and antique. • Secure to page with foam dots, adding silhouette photos. • Punch shadow alphabet in Copper foil and alphabet in Aluminum foil. Add rough texture with stylus and antique. • Run all letters through Xyron. Press alphabet on shadow and secure letters at an angle to page.

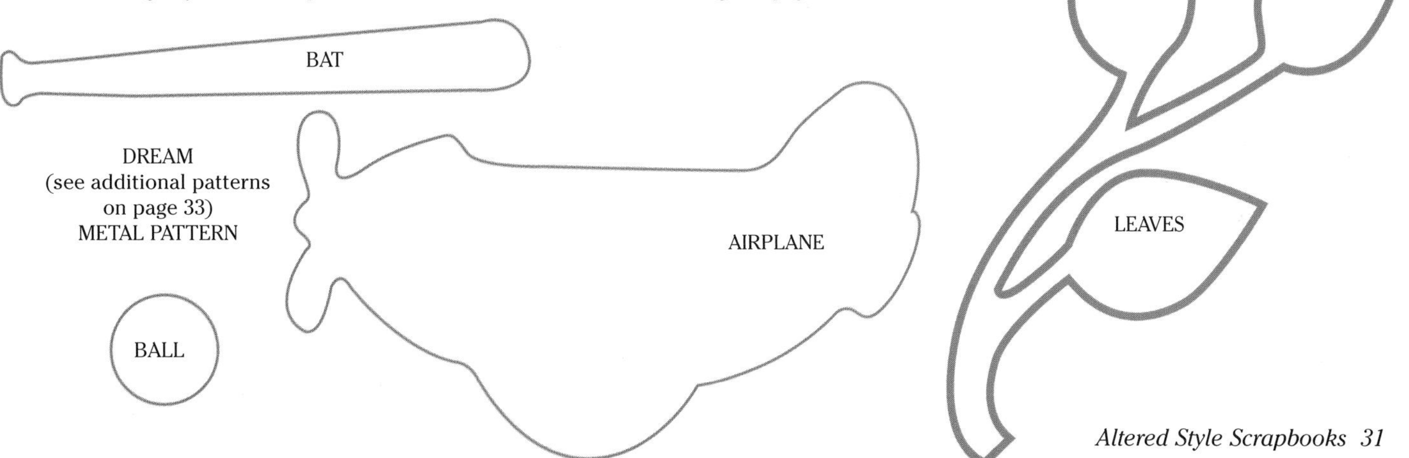

SWIMMING LESSONS

by Shirley Rufener

MATERIALS: *Design Originals* Legacy Collage Papers (#0532 Red Patterns, #0539 Plaid Hanky) • *K & S Metals* 36-gauge Aluminum tooling foil & Aluminum mesh • Cardstock (Blue, Gray, White) • *Sizzix* die-cutter (Dies: Rectangle Frame #38-0163, Tags #38-0236, Splats #38-0192 & Confetti #38-0148) • *Tsukineko StazOn* ink pads (Ultramarine, Blazing Red) • 5 Blue 'E' beads • 3" piece of White cording • *Xyron* machine with permanent adhesive • Adhesive foam dots • *Leather Factory* 1/4" alphabet/number leather stamp set • Fine point permanent Black marker • Double-sided adhesive tape • *Aleene's* Memory Glue • *EK Success* Tracer Templates: Block Uppercase & Funky ABC • Retracted twist-style ink pen • Brayer • Wood stylus tool (pointed wood stick or dowel) • Mallet • Pink and Black craft foam sheet • *Fiskars* Metalworks Scissors & Bubbles Paper Edger scissors

INSTRUCTIONS: Die-cut 3 foil frames and use left-over 'openings' for two of them. • Cut one with Paper Edgers and another with Metalworks Scissors. • Round corners on large frame. • Cut 1/4" off all sides of last die-cut frame. • Gently tap larger end of pen with mallet to emboss circles on frames. • Smooth frame with brayer.

Shaker Window: Die-cut one foil and one black foam tag leaving 1/2" on all sides. • Cut 3/4" wide frames using left-over 'openings'. • Cut mesh, craft plastic and Red Patterns paper slightly smaller than outer frame edge. • Cut a small swim board from pink foam using inner shape of arched window pattern. • Thread beads on cording. • Glue both embellishments to mesh. • Secure mesh to paper and foam and foil over mesh using tape.

Embellishments: Die-cut one foil Splats and three Confetti designs. • Stamp emboss date numbers on Splat. • Impress a line on confetti circles with stylus. • Emboss 'SPLASH' with Funky template letters onto foil. • Antique word and textured frames, 3 confetti swirls and 2 dots with Ultramarine. • Save extra 5 shapes for a future project. • Trace title in pencil then marker. • Chalk blue. • Mat title on foil and glue dots to sides. • Color two rectangles of mesh Red. • Secure mesh with tape. • Secure splats and confetti to mesh with foam dots.

Aging and Color Tinting Paper

1. To age papers, apply decorating chalk with a circular motion.

2. To color tint an area, lightly apply chalk with applicator. Mistakes are erasable.

SPLASH
METAL
PATTERNS

SCHOOL DAYS

by Susan Keuter

MATERIALS: *Design Originals* Legacy Collage Paper (#0541 Report Card) • *Bazzill* cardstock (Cream, Tan, Brown) • *Ink It!* (glass slide, Copper tape, Copper plant tag) • *Robin's Nest* glassine envelopes • *American Tag* brads

INSTRUCTIONS: Glue envelopes to Report Card paper. • Insert journaling into envelopes. • Mat photo on Cream, Brown and Tan cardstock. • Glue to page. • Cut and tear words from patterned paper, place in slide. • Attach plant tag with brads, glue slide in place.

Make a frame around a glass or plastic slide with Copper foil tape.

Make a textured Copper plate.

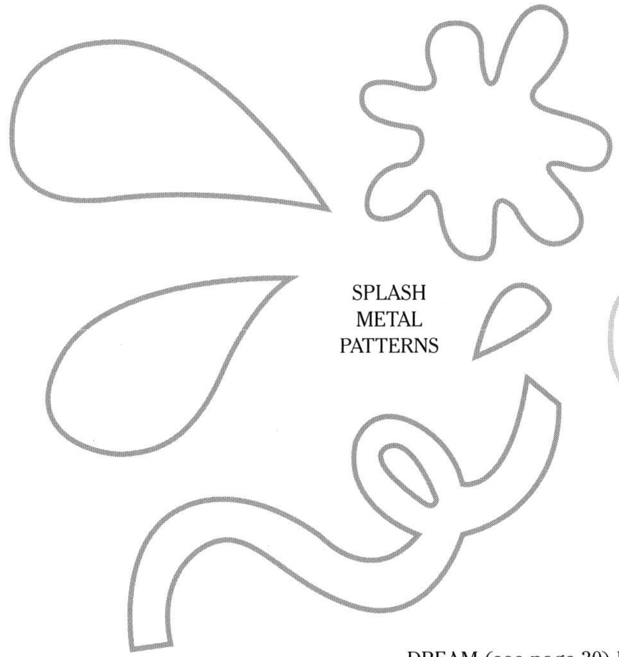

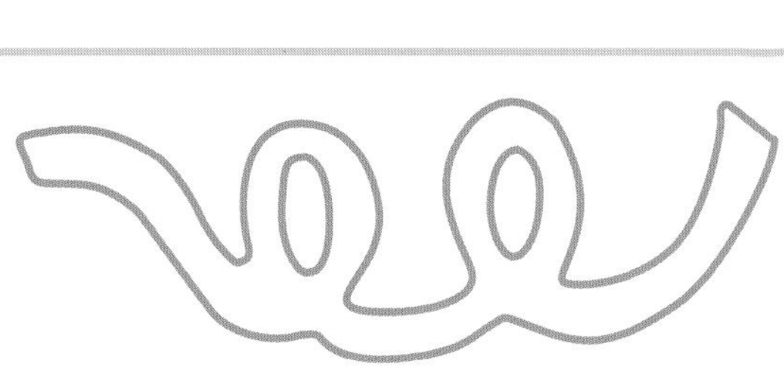

SCHOOL DAYS METAL PATTERNS

SPLASH METAL PATTERNS

SCHOOL DAYS METAL PATTERNS

DREAM (see page 30) METAL PATTERN

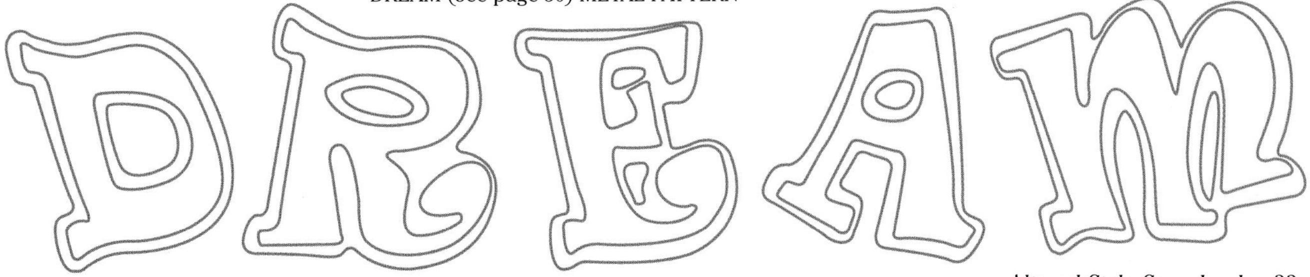

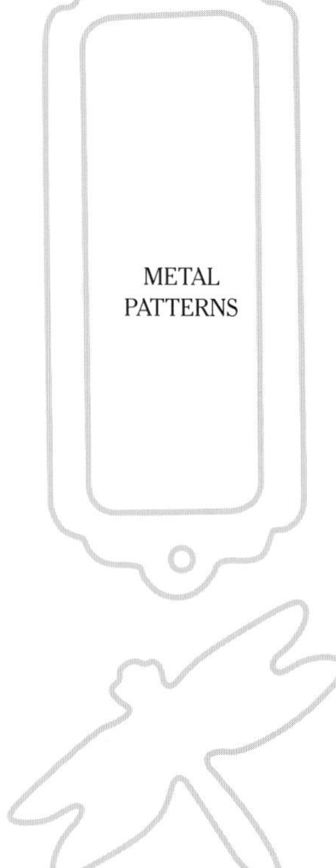

You'll Love This Fabulous Window and Niche Album! Dimensional Flowers Are Visible on Every Page!

NICHE ALBUM *by Shirley Rufener*

MATERIALS: *Design Originals* Legacy Collage Papers (2 each #0534 Ruth's Violets, #0536 Violets Hanky, #0537 Faces of Friends) • Cardstock (Ivory, Lavender, White) • Ivory parchment paper • *K & S Metals* 36-gauge Copper tooling foil • Eyelets (2 Silver 1/8", 22 Brown 3/16") • Eyelet setter • Mallet or hammer • *Ellison Sizzix* die-cutter (Photo Corners die #38-0145 & Dragonfly die #38-0232) • *Quickutz* personal die-cutting machine (Hat & Tag die) • *Tsukineko StazOn* Timber Brown ink pad • Large needle • *Aleene's* Memory Glue & Paper Glaze • *Xyron* machine with permanent adhesive • Mini adhesive foam dots • X-Acto blade knife • Metal ruler • 3/16" and 1/8" hole punches

ALBUM COVER INSTRUCTIONS: Remove wire binding and glue Ruth's Violets paper to front of covers. • Hold covers up to a light source and prick hole placement with needle. Re-punch holes with 3/16" hole punch. • Secure paper to inside of covers. • Die-cut two tags from foil and cut off 1/4" at bottom of each. • Die-cut a dragonfly and 4 photo corners from foil. • Emboss details and antique all shapes. • When ink dries, set a Silver eyelet in each tag hole. • Center tags and glue on album cover, with straight edges together. • Set Brown eyelets in album cover holes. • Curve dragonfly wings and secure. • Glue Ivory cardstock title and 3 rhinestone flowers.

ALBUM PAGE INSTRUCTIONS: Age album pages. • Trace frame pattern opening, 5/8" from top right corner of the first 7 album pages with pencil. • Cut openings of first 6 pages only with X-Acto. • Layer flowers motif from Violets Hanky papers in 3-D, inside 7th page niche area. Erase square. • Trace and cut a window from cardstock. • Cut openings with X-Acto, and cover window with Faces of Friends paper. • Glue window over niche of first album page. • Trace 11 more windows onto Faces paper. • Cut out one, including openings. • Glue to the back side of first page. • Cut frame only of remaining windows (no cross-bars), and secure to both sides of 5 niche-marked pages. • Collage matted photos, torn printed paper, die-cuts, wedding quotes and embellishments and glue in place.

3-D Paper Layering

Three dimensional decoupage has been around for years. Only recently have scrapbookers translated this craft for use in their memory albums by using dimensional foam dots between paper layers.

1. With small pointed scissors cut 2 of the same motif from paper and foreground elements.

2. Cut away any visible background with X-Acto knife. Clip and shape elements.

3. Glue solid design to project. Adhere middle layer with mini foam dots.

4. Secure final layer with foam dots, apply Paper Glaze to visible designs.

Open to page 1 to see through the window frame. There's a dimensional flower bouquet inside the window.

Open to page 2 to see the window frame on the left, with flowers peeking through the panes. Look through the square window on the right to see the dimensional flower bouquet.

Open to page 3 to see the window frame on the left, with flowers still showing through. The window frame is still visible on the right side. These pages are ready to decorate with collage papers and photos.

Open to page 4 to see the window frame on the left. On the right you'll see the dimensional flowers.
Note: The dimensional flowers have been protected in the window niche.

GRANDMA'S NOTIONS

by Shirley Rufener

MATERIALS: *Design Originals* Legacy Collage Paper (#0530 Mom's Sewing Box) • Two 5" x 7" wood frames with flat surface • *Aleene's* Wood Glue, Instant Decoupage (Gloss), Memory Glue, 7800 Adhesive • Black acrylic paint • *StazOn* Timber Brown ink pad • Foam applicator brush • *K & S Metals* 36-gauge Aluminum tooling foil • *Sizzix* die-cutter (scissors die-cut #38-0144) • Found objects or memorabilia (buttons, hooks, etc.) • *Tsukineko* Dauber tool

INSTRUCTIONS: Coordinate background paper with frame designs. • Plan positions before gluing anything in place. • Paint frames black with foam applicator. • Decoupage small paper cutouts and add a final coating of Instant Decoupage to finish and seal images. • Secure glass in top frame. • Die-cut scissors and age with ink. • Use Memory Glue for plastic, cloth or paper items. Use 7800 for metal objects and objects to be glued onto the wood frame itself.

RODNEY'S ADVENTURES

by Shirley Rufener

MATERIALS: *Design Originals* Legacy Collage Papers (#0540 Skates, #0543 Brushes) • *Sizzix* die-cutter (camera die #38-0141) • *Aleene's* Paper Glaze • Bronze seed beads • Foam dots

INSTRUCTIONS: Glue Skates paper to back of frame. • Glue Brushes paper to 3" x 4" cardboard and mount with foam dots. • Adhere photo with foam dots. • Glue camera die-cut and seed beads.

Shadow Box Variations

• For a fun variation, try making a set of Sepia tone photos framed in aged metal belt buckles. Cut the buckle away from the strap, remove latch with pliers. Secure photo to back of buckle with 7800 adhesive. Mount photos with foam dots onto an aged paper background. Make tiny name plaques with leather stamps on tooling foil. Age the metal. Die cut foil photo corners (Sizzix die #38-0145). Emboss with tiny spirals, age foil and secure to frame corners with 7800.

• Another idea is to use a photo embellished with scanned memorabilia. It's fun if you don't have an item to find an image of it online or in a magazine. You can add to the realism by applying Paper Glaze to the image. Attach image with foam dots for dimension.

• Coordinate background paper with frame designs. Plan positions before gluing anything in place. Paint frames with a foam applicator brush. Decoupage small paper cutouts. Add a final coating of Instant Decoupage to finish and seal images. Secure glass in top frame. Use Memory Glue for plastic, cloth or paper items. Use 7800 for metal objects and objects to be glued onto the wood frame itself.

Memorabilia Shadow Boxes

The wonderful dimension of shadow boxes make them perfect for embellishing with 3-D objects and memorabilia. You can make them yourself from two plain frames.

1. Remove glass and easel mat from two matching frames.

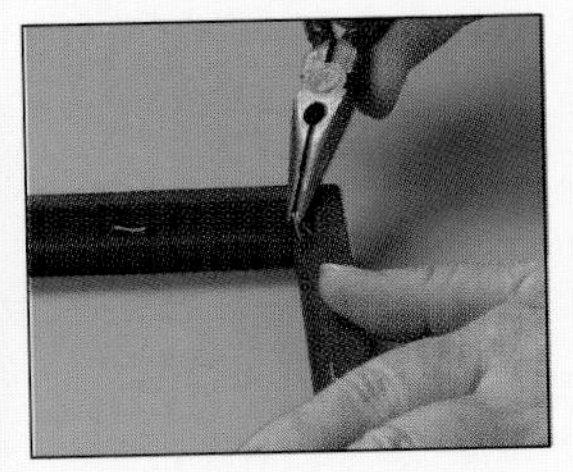

2. Remove staples from top frame only with pliers. Paint both frames and decorate the top one, if desired.

3. Permanently secure glass in top frame with a thin line of 7800 adhesive. Dry flat.

4. Sand bottom surface of top frame. Stack and glue frames, both facing up, with Aleene's wood glue.

5. Glue background paper to mat, create collage. Reinsert mat, secure in frame.

THE MORRIS BOYS

by Susan Keuter

MATERIALS: *Design Originals* Legacy Collage Paper (#0550 TeaDye Script) • Cardstock (*Bazzill* Ecru, Tan; *DMD* French Vanilla) • *Accu-Cut* tag die-cut • *All My Memories* Typewriter Keys letter stickers • *Sharon Soneff/C.I.* Flea Market sticker letters • *Making Memories* (pewter word & eyelet, square page pebble) • Twine • *Hero Arts* Playful lettering stamp • *ColorBox* Cat's Eye Chestnut Roan chalking ink

INSTRUCTIONS: For photo mat tear French Vanilla to size. • Cut TeaDye Script to size for page. • For Script mats cut Ecru cardstock. • Arrange on page. • Stamp words on tag. • Collage tag with TeaDye Script, pewter word, eyelet, page pebble and small stickers. • Tie twine to tag, apply to page. • Write name with Typewriter Keys stickers • Add words with Flea Market stickers.

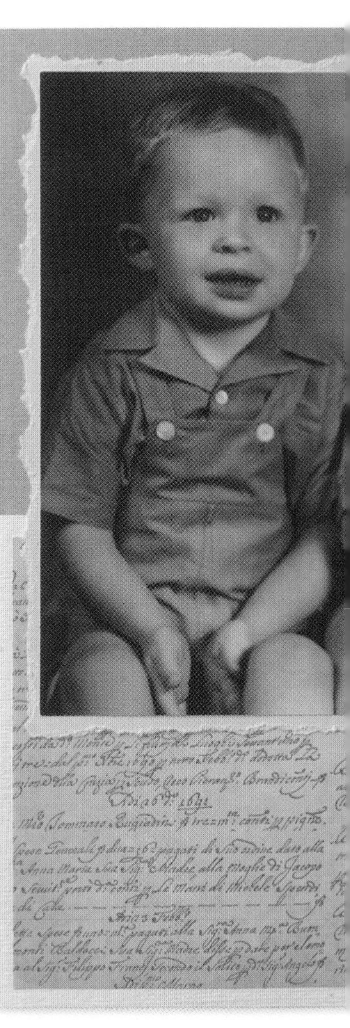

The Protective Envelope Around the Photo Opens to Reveal a Beautiful Young Woman!

JenNY *by Renée Plains*

MATERIALS: *Design Originals* Legacy Collage Paper (#0551 Legacy Words, #0495 Brown floral) • Vintage photo holder with photo • *EK Success* Fresh Cuts "Love Notes" sticker • Letter tiles • 6 Cream buttons • Taupe ribbon • Small rustic star • Round paper clip • 6" piece of wire • Chalk

INSTRUCTIONS: Adhere $2^1/2$" strip of Legacy Words paper to bottom of Brown floral paper. • Type 'remembering grandmother Jenny on her wedding day', cut apart words and glue on page. • Glue all elements on page. • Use chalk to age as desired.

ANDY *by Delores Frantz*
MATERIALS: *Design Originals* Legacy Collage Paper (#0538 Peter's Dreams, #0479 Green stripe, #0496 TeaDye alphabet, #0499 TeaDye music) • *Design Originals* Legacy Cut (#0504 Holiday) • *ColorBox* Cat's Eye Chestnut Roan chalking ink • 1 Large square & 8 round eyelets • Eyelet setter • 2 1/8" x 5 1/4" Tag • 8" Fiber • 1/8" & 1/4" Circle punches • Hammer
INSTRUCTIONS: Cut scroll designs, letters and numbers from TeaDye alphabet paper. • Tear image from Peter's Dream paper, cut 4 holiday cuts. • Age all edges with chalk. • Assemble page. • Secure letters and numbers with round eyelets. • Secure tag with square eyelet, attach fiber.

IMAGINE *by Delores Frantz*
MATERIALS: *Design Originals* Legacy Collage Paper (#0526 Two Ladies, #0482 Teal stripe, #0483 Teal floral) • Peach cardstock • *ColorBox* Cat's Eye Chestnut Roan chalking ink • 18" of 20-gauge craft wire • Wire phrase 'imagine' • Alphabet letter beads • 1 1/4" Heart charm • Goop adhesive
INSTRUCTIONS: Mat Teal stripe paper on cardstock. • Mat photo on Teal floral, then to cardstock. • Tear 2 Ladies from collage paper. • Glue ladies, then photo to page. • Attach 'imagine' to page with brads or wire. • Use Goop to glue alphabet bead words together. • When dry, thread onto wire 1 word at a time bending loops in wire between words. • Glue words and charm to page.

SEW WHAT

by Susan Keuter

MATERIALS: *Design Originals* Legacy Collage Paper (#0532 Red Patterns) • *Bazzill* cardstock (Hunter Green, Ecru, Black) • *Paper Adventure* Antique Gold paper • Green eyelets • *Scrapyard 326* metal letters • *ThermOWeb* Zots metal adhesive • *May Arts* Green chenille yarn • *Stampin' Up!* Antique Gold embossing powder • Fabric scraps

INSTRUCTIONS: Journal on Ecru cardstock; attach 'Sew' near top of words. • Mat words on Gold paper. • Type words to go under photo. • Cut out and edge with embossing powder. • Set eyelets in top corners. • Run yarn through eyelets. • Mat photo on White cardstock. • Cut Black cardstock longer than photo, tear bottom edge. • Mat photo on Black, then Green. • Glue fabric scrap and words to Black mat edge. • Assemble page.

FRIENDS *by Susan Keuter*

MATERIALS: *Design Originals* Legacy Collage Paper (#0547 Dictionary) • *Bazzill* cardstock (Ivory, Red, Blue) • *Making Memories* Ransom eyelet letters • *Craf-T* chalk • *ThermOWeb* Zots

INSTRUCTIONS: Cut strips of Red and Blue cardstock, overlap and glue. • Mat 3 photos on joined piece. • On Ivory cardstock, type journaling and words for title. • Cut out and rub edges with very Light Beige chalk. • Rub selected words with Red and Blue chalk. • Set metal letters on title piece with Zots. • Assemble page.

CHEAP SEATS

by Susan Keuter

MATERIALS: *Design Originals* Legacy Collage Paper (#0555 Tags) • *Bazzill* cardstock (Ivory, Pale Yellow, Light Green) • Dusty Rose corrugated paper • *Diane's Ribbons* netting • *American Fastener* brads • *Avery* shipping tag • 5" Hemp • Date stamp • *Stampin' Up* ink & chalk

INSTRUCTIONS: Mat Tags paper on Light Green cardstock. • Type title and journaling on Pale Yellow cardstock. • Stamp date on tag, tear bottom off. • Loop hemp through tag hole. • Tear the 2 long edges of title piece. • Attach netting to Tags paper. • Attach title with glue and brad. • Mat photo on White and Green cardstock, then on corrugated paper. • Attach to page with glue and brad. • Add tag and journaling to page.

HANNAH AND JOHN

by Susan Keuter

MATERIALS: *Design Originals* Legacy Collage Papers (#0548 Passport, #0551 Legacy Words, #0487 Rust linen) • *Bazzill* cardstock (Brown, Dark Brown) • *Making Memories* Pewter letters & eyelets (quotes, letters, shapes) • Brads • *Sharon Soneff* Flea Market letter stickers • *Timeless Tapestry* Autumn Leaves fiber

INSTRUCTIONS: Mat Legacy Words on Brown cardstock, 1 large and 3 small pieces. • On larger matted piece, attach fiber with brads; center pewter quote over fiber. • Write names with eyelets across 2 of the smaller matted pieces. • Add number stickers for date. • Print words on Rust linen paper. • Attach heart eyelet to a piece of Rust linen. • Mat a photo on Brown cardstock then Passport paper. • Assemble page.

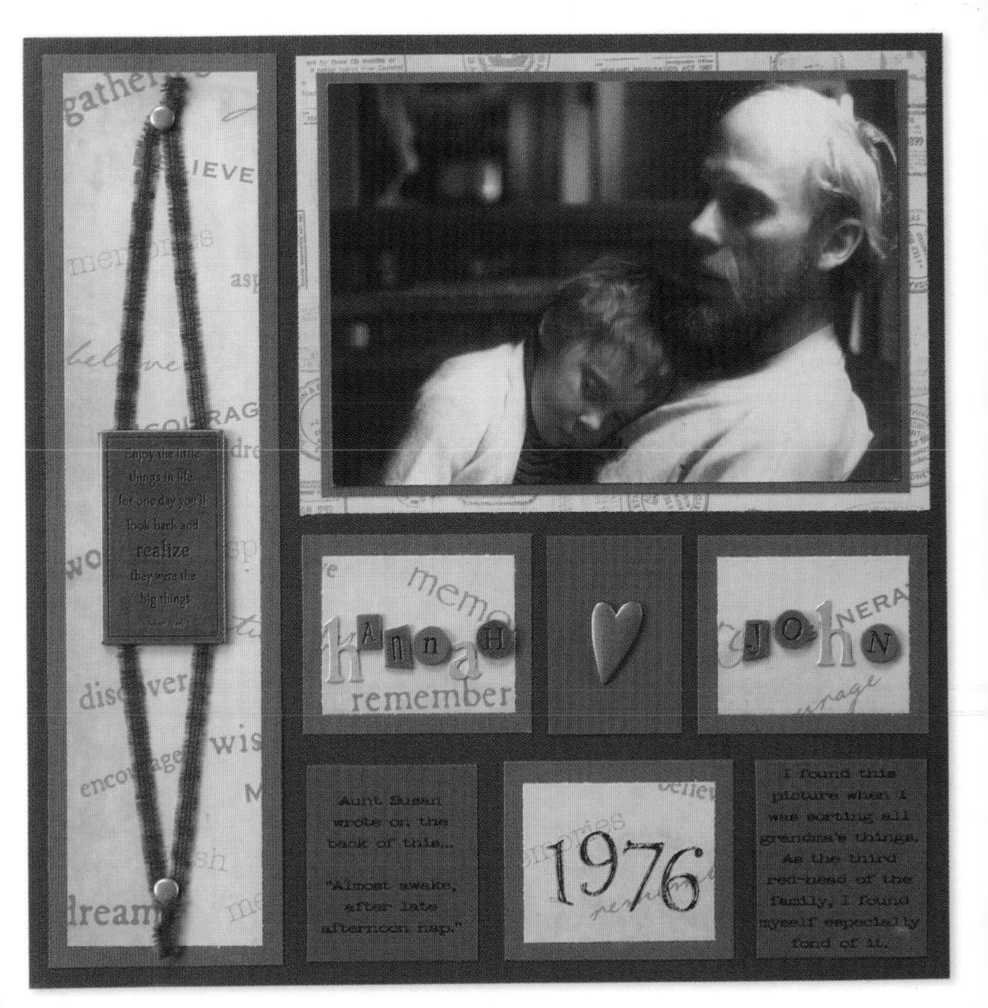

Our friends have their family picture taken during their summer vacation in the mountains every year. I wanted to show how they've changed over the past years so I made a folder to keep some of their pictures together.

THOMPSON FAMILY

by Mary Kaye Seckler

MATERIALS: Forest Green cardstock • *Stickabilities* gold adhesive letters • *AlphaBetterLetter* Template • *7 Gypsies* Gold clasp • *On the Surface* Gold metallic thread

INSTRUCTIONS: Crop all the photos the same size. • Trace and score the middle photo dimensions in the center of the cardstock. • Score a 1/8" gutter on all four sides of the photo. • Trace the photo again to the right and left of the middle photo, and above and below. • Cut out the shape you have traced; adhere the photos. • With the folder closed, trace the years using the stencil and a Black pen on each of the four flaps. • Add the title in Gold letters to the front. • Make the clasp by tying Gold thread through the holes at the side of the two clasp parts. • Tighten the thread and knot. Trim the ends.

Magic with Journaling

I have a curiosity about the past. I want to know where I came from and what circumstances made me the way I am. I hear snippets of family gossip whispered and my curiosity is piqued. If my legacy hadn't been preserved for me in some way - through family scrapbooks, journaling, stories and diaries, I dig through dusty attics and damp basements. I find old shoeboxes of photos and make guesses as to the identity of the strangers within. I need answers.

I scrapbook for the same reasons you might keep a journal - to remind myself of the progress I make in life. Not just the milestones I pass, but hopefully, the way I improve with age, the lessons I learn, the choices I make. A scrapbook is a concrete way to reassure ourselves that we're on the right track. I sometimes gather up a group of photos and think to myself that the occasion was not my finest hour. I record the event anyway, as truthfully as possible. It is evidence of the reality we live in.

Mary Kaye Seckler

DESTINATION HARVARD

by Susan Keuter

MATERIALS: *Design Originals* Legacy Collage Paper (#0554 Diamonds) • *Bazzill* cardstock (Ecru, Tan, Light Brown, Burgundy) • 2" x 2" Black slide mounts • *Avery* jewelry tag • *Doodlebug Designs* Fancypants letter stickers • *Making Memories* Simply Stated rub-on words • *Marvy* Giga Punch square punch • Burgundy sewing thread

INSTRUCTIONS: Mat photo on Burgundy cardstock. • Print words on Ecru and Tan. • Cut squares around words. • Mount Ecru words behind slide mounts. • Press title on Light Brown cardstock. • Sew slide mounts and Tan word squares through Diamonds paper. • Glue Tan square onto photo, glue photo in place. • Attach tag to title, glue to page.

CABIN 53 *by Renée Plains*

MATERIALS: *Design Originals* Legacy Collage Papers (#0547 Dictionary, #0551 Legacy Words, #0555 Tags, #0492 Coffee floral) • Tan cardstock • 2" x 2" White slide mounts • *Mrs Grossman's* Vellum Medallion stickers • *EK Success* Fresh Cuts FC030 Love Notes sticker • *Ma Vinci's Reliquary* number rubber stamps • *Postmodern Designs* walnut ink • Star charm • Round paper clip • Small envelope • Decorating chalks

INSTRUCTIONS: Cut 12" x 8" Coffee floral paper with deckle scissors; glue to cardstock. • Cut out "memories" and "the past" from Legacy Words paper, age then glue in place. • Cover slide mounts with aged Dictionary paper. • Arrange elements and glue on page. • Age as desired with chalk or walnut ink.

BLESSED *by Renée Plains*

MATERIALS: *Design Originals* Legacy Collage Papers (#0542 Farm House, #0545 Ledger) • 2" x 2" White slide mounts • Color copy of an old calendar • *EK Success* Nostalgiques by Rebecca Sower tag and label holder stickers • *Making Memories* 'blessed' definition sticker • Rubber stamps (*Stamp La Jolla* #619 449-4600 heart; *PSX* #B-3244 heart; *Inkadinkado* 'sweet') • Eyelets • Striped ribbon and small button

INSTRUCTIONS: Glue photocopy of calendar and large photo in place. • Place tag and definition (aged with walnut ink) stickers on page. • Stamp words and affix tags, stickers and elements to page with eyelets. Affix eyelets in tag holes. • Cover slide frames with Farm House paper, age with chalk, place photo behind frame and glue in place. • Sew ribbon and button on.

ROSE AND HENRY *by Renée Plains*

MATERIALS: *Design Originals* Legacy Collage Papers (#0539 Plaid Hanky, #0542 Farm House, #0551 Legacy Words) • *Design Originals* Transparency Sheet (#0556 Word Tags) • 2" x 2" White slide mount • *ColorBox* Cat's Eye chalking inks • *My Mind's Eye* "Fresh Fabrics" Red Stars frame and buttons clip • Photo of young woman and photo booth strip • Flower stickers • 3 *Scrapbook Interiors* round nailheads • Vintage labels and found objects

INSTRUCTIONS: Glue picture in stars frame and place on page. • Glue photo strip on frame. • Cut words from Legacy Words paper, chalk to age, then glue in place. • Punch two squares from paper stamped with script and attach to page with round top nails. • Insert transparency in slide mount aged with chalk ink. • Cut a rectangle from Farm House paper and glue to page; glue button clips to this. • Place flower stickers on page.

Slide Mounts

Create clever little frames!

MATERIALS: *Design Originals* Transparency Sheet (#0556 Word Tags) • White slide mount • *ColorBox* Cat's Eyes chalking ink or powdered chalk

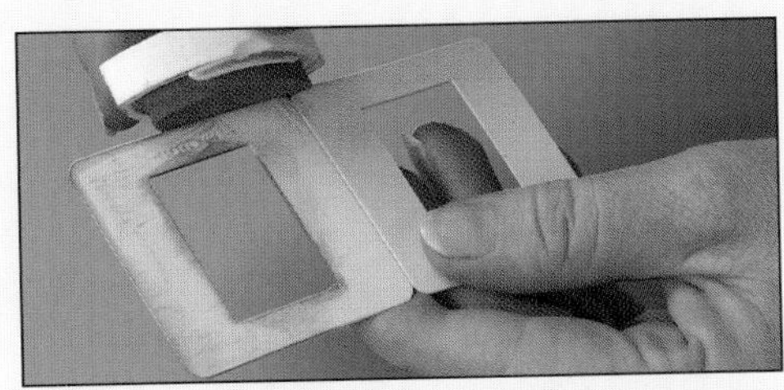

Age edges with chalking ink.

Apply chalk to front of slide mount.

WISH *by Renée Plains*

MATERIALS: *Design Originals* Legacy Collage Papers (#0526 Two Ladies, #0549 Shorthand) • *Design Originals* Transparency Sheet (#0556 Word Tags) • 2" x 2" round slide mount • Old vintage album frame with photo • Two small envelopes aged with Walnut Ink • Old button card with buttons • *Rubbermoon* 'xoxo' rubber stamp • Jewelry tag • Vintage label • Buttons • *Making Memories* 'wish' definition sticker • *EK Success* Nostalgiques by Rebecca Sower tag sticker • Vintage watch crystal • *Artchix Studio* star nailhead • Wire

INSTRUCTIONS: Cut out two half circles for arch from Two Ladies paper, chalk to age, then glue in place. • Glue old frame with picture below arch. • Dip envelopes in walnut ink to age and glue in place. • Add wire with jewelry tag and button card to envelopes. • Write 'wish' on label and glue on frame. • Insert 'Wish' transparency in slide mount aged with chalk. • Place tag sticker on page, affix nail head on frame and watch crystal on arch.• Cut rectangles from Two Ladies paper; glue remaining elements on page.

Pocket Envelope

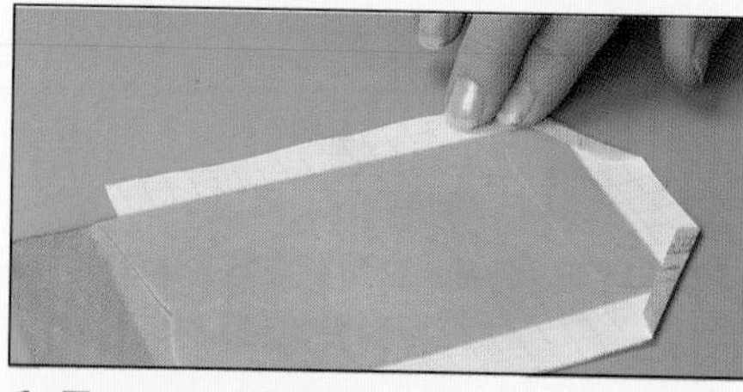

1. Trace and cut out envelope.

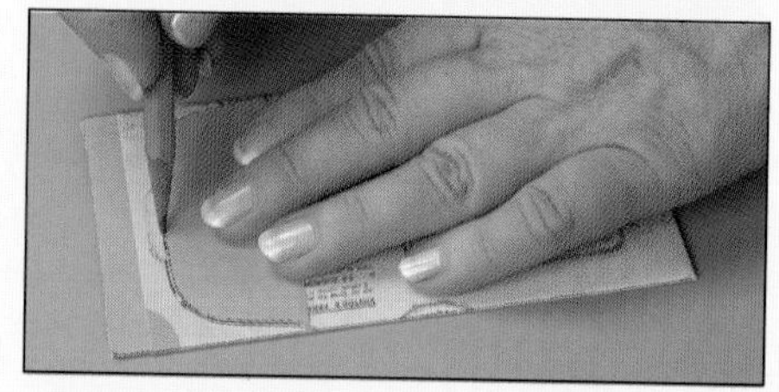

2. Cover envelope with paper.

GOOD TO HAVE AN END

by Mary Kaye Seckler

MATERIALS: *Design Originals* Legacy Collage Paper (#0543 Brushes) • $4\frac{1}{4}$" x $5\frac{1}{4}$" card • *Judikins* coin envelope template • *On the Surface* fibers • Rubber Stamps (*Stampin' Up* map background, 'Congrats!'; *Stampers Anonymous* #G3-824 'It is good to have an end') • Ink pads (*Marvy* Brown, *ColorBox* Chestnut Cat's Eye chalking ink • *Deluxe Cuts* tag template

INSTRUCTIONS: Stamp map background on cardstock. Edge the card in Chestnut chalking ink. • Trace the coin envelope onto Brushes paper; cut out. Score and fold, glue flaps and attach to card with a glue stick. • Trace the tag template onto cardstock and cut out. Stamp 'It is good to have an end...' on the tag. • Punch a hole and thread fibers through. Insert the tag into the envelope. • Stamp 'Congrats!' on the inside of card.

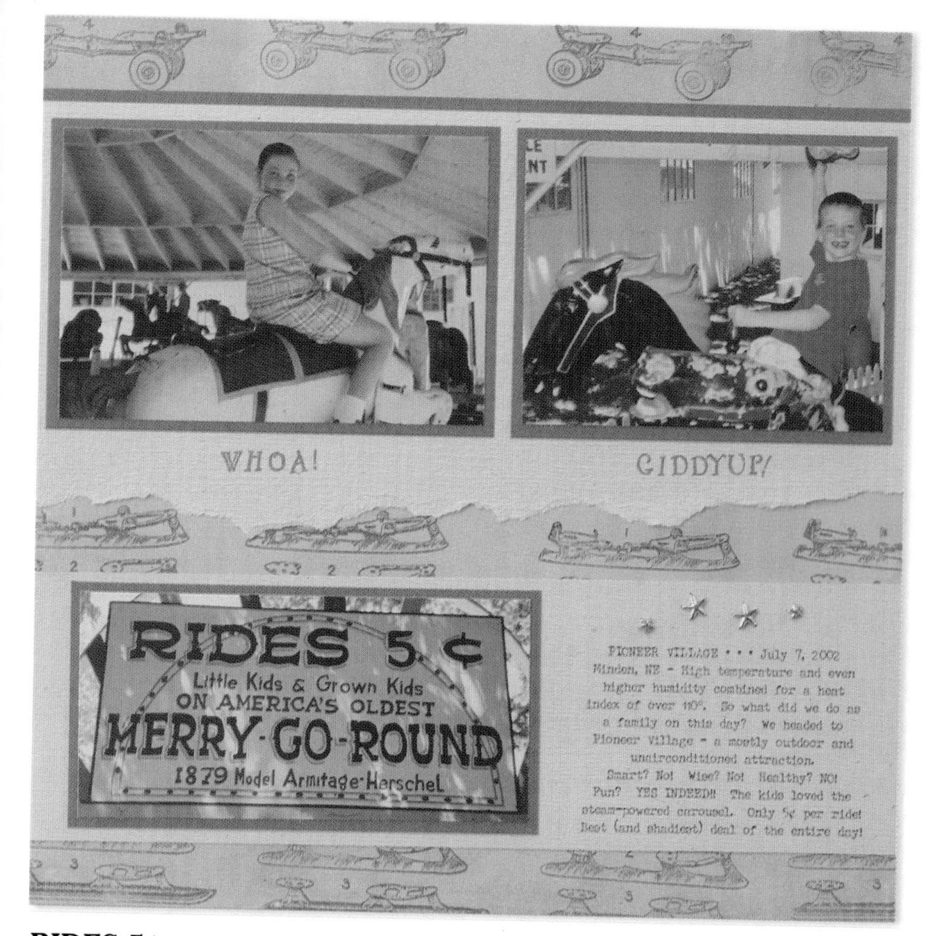

RIDES 5¢ *by Susan Keuter*

MATERIALS: *Design Originals* Legacy Collage Paper (#0540 Skates) • *Bazzill* Cappuccino cardstock • *DMD* French Vanilla paper • *Scrapbook Barn* Silver nailhead stars • *Hero Arts* Playful stamp lettering • *ColorBox* Cat's Eye Chestnut Roan chalking ink

INSTRUCTIONS: Mat photos on Cappuccino cardstock. • Print journaling on right side of French Vanilla paper; glue photo on strip. • Set stars over words. • Attach to Skates paper. • Tear one edge of French Vanilla wide enough for 2 photos. • Mat top of paper with Cappuccino, attach photos and glue to Skates paper. • Stamp words under photos.

SHRINE CARD

by Mary Kaye Seckler

MATERIALS: *Design Originals* Legacy Collage Paper (#0549 Shorthand) • Cardstock (Cream, Copper $8\frac{1}{2}$" x $5\frac{1}{2}$" folded in half) • *AccuCut* shrine die-cut • 1 piece Brown Bird's Nest • 2 pieces Cream paper • 2 Copper eyelets • *On the Surface* Copper thread • 1 Copper key • Rubber stamps (*Stampin Up'* 'Best Wishes'; *Hampton Art Stamps* 'Art washes away') • *ColorBox* Chestnut Cat's Eye chalking ink • Double-stick mounting tape

INSTRUCTIONS: Die-cut shrine from Shorthand paper backed with Cream cardstock. • Die-cut shrine from Shorthand paper for inside of shrine. • Edge die-cuts with Chestnut chalking ink. • Adhere unbacked Shorthand shrine to Copper card. • Cut doorway in backed shrine. Score vertical lines and fold the doors open. • Edge the doorway in Chestnut chalking ink and set eyelets into the doors. • Adhere piece of bird's nest in shrine opening. • Stamp 'Art washes away' on Cream paper, tear edges, edge with Chestnut chalking ink and glue on bird's nest. • Attach front shrine piece with double-stick mounting tape. • Thread metallic thread with Copper key through eyelets and tie. • Stamp 'Best Wishes' on cream paper, tear edges, crumple paper and age with Chestnut chalking ink. • Attach the paper to the card using double-stick mounting tape.

Alter Paper

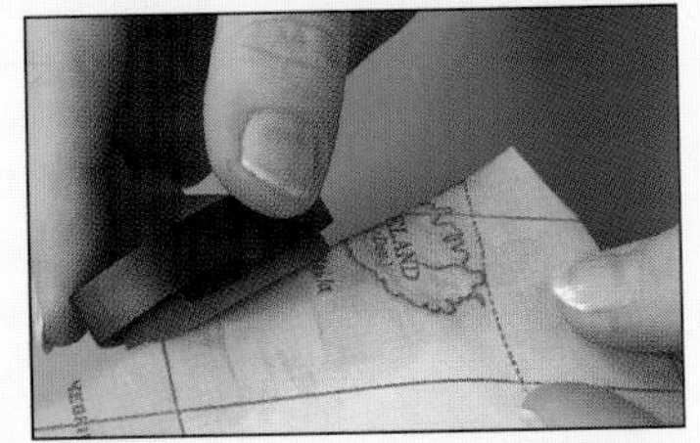

Sponge background paper with glazes.

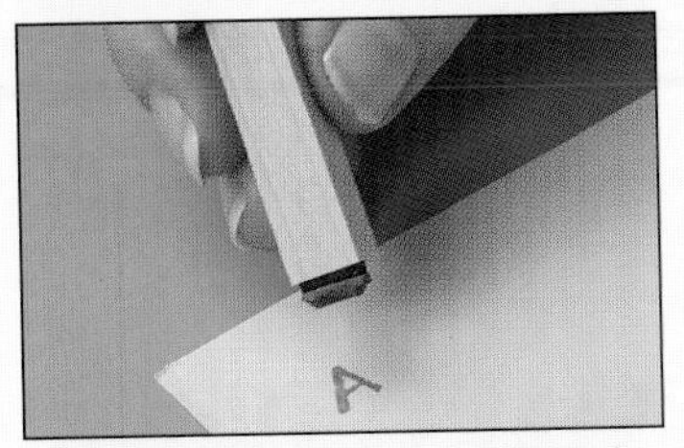

Edge paper with an ink pad.

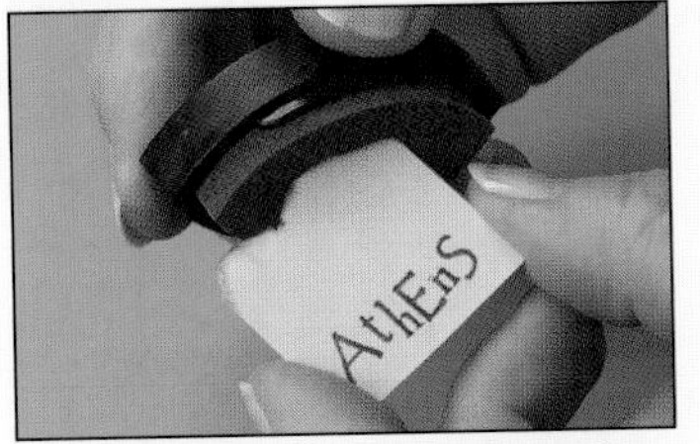

Stamp titles on cardstock.

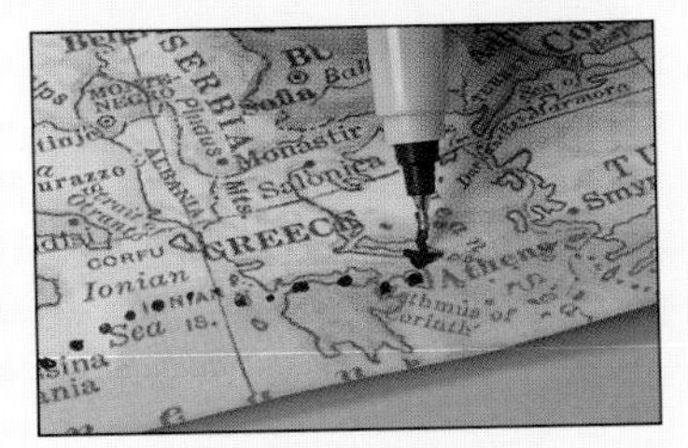

Tint edges with ink pad.

Mark route with dots.

DESTINATION ATHENS *by Mary Kaye Seckler*

MATERIALS: *Design Originals* Legacy Collage Papers (#0548 Passport, #0553 Map) • Aqua cardstock • *Golden* glazes (Patina Green, Seafoam Green) • Sea sponge • Rubber Stamps (*Limited Edition* Greek passport; *Hero Arts* Good Alphabet, Printer's Lowercase Alphabets, December Mark, Luxe Cancellation) • Ink pads (*ColorBox* Cat's Eye Harbor, Teal, Robin's Egg, Topaz and Chestnut; *Marvy* Ochre & Teal) • *Scrappy's* Brass label frame • *Deluxe Cuts* #1P & #2T tag template • 1/4" White eyelet • One 1" White tag • Gold brads • Map scrap • *On the Surface* fibers • Black marker • *Foofala* Foofabets in two sizes

INSTRUCTIONS: Sponge Patina Green glaze around edges of Map paper; let dry. • Sponge Seafoam Green glaze over Patina Green; let dry. • Tint edges with Harbor chalking ink. • Stamp 'Athens' on Ivory cardstock, tear edge, insert in gold frame and affix to page with brads. • Mark journey with Black dots. • Trace tag template on Aqua cardstock; cut out. • Attach map piece to tag end; edge with Teal chalking ink. • Set eyelet in tag; insert fibers. • Trim 'Destination' letters from Foofabets; edge with Robin's Egg chalking ink and glue to tag. • Rubber stamp and attach ephemera to tag; adhere to page. • Trace pocket envelope template onto Passport paper; score, cut out and glue together. • Edge pocket with Topaz & Chestnut chalking inks. • Tint 1" tag with Ochre; stamp 'tickets' in Ochre ink. • Rubber stamp and adhere ephemera to pocket. • Attach 'ticket' tag to pocket with brad. • Adhere pocket to page. • Mat photos with Aqua cardstock and place on page.

Make a Tag with Letters for the Title

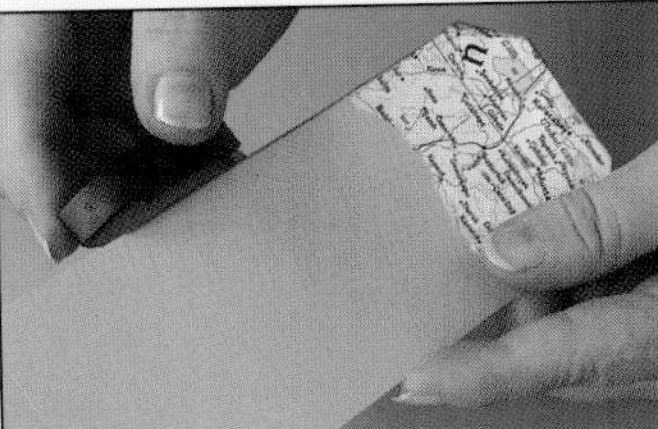

1. Glue map piece on tag.

2. Tint edges with ink pad.

3. Glue letter blocks on tag.

4. Rubber stamp postal cancellations on tag.

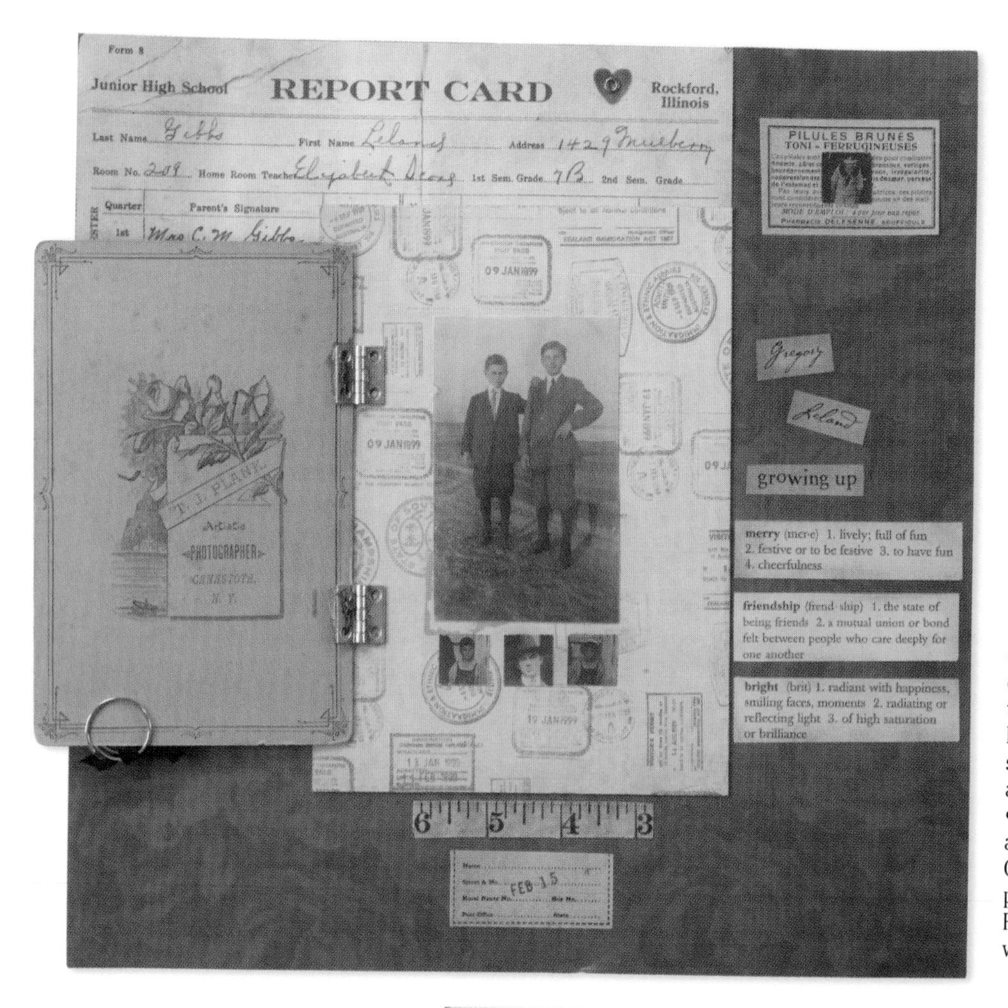

REPORT CARD

by Renée Plains

MATERIALS: *Design Originals* Legacy Collage Papers (#0541 Report Card, #0548 Passport, #0495 Brown floral) • Vintage photo card and small photos • *Making Memories* Defined Stickers ('bright', 'merry', 'friendship' definitions) • *EK Success* Nostalgiques by Rebecca Sower stickers (tag, typewriter keys and label) • 2 small hinges • Small piece of tape measure • Postage stamps • Round paper clip • Ribbon • *Artchix Studio* pharmacy label • 1/2" heart punch • Copper mesh • Eyelet • Chalk

INSTRUCTIONS: Adhere torn report card to Brown floral paper. • Cut two cone hats from Report Card paper, chalk to age and glue in place with typewriter key stickers on hats. • Glue Passport paper to cardboard; cut to size and attach hinges to photo card and Passport paper. • Adhere to page. • Type words on computer; cut apart and glue in place; age with chalk. • Glue elements on page. • Tie ribbon on paper clip and place on photo card. • Punch mesh heart and affix to page with eyelet.

Open the Photo to Reveal Another Group of Family Photos.

Embellish the Page with Found Objects, Hinges, Paper Clips, Dictionary Words, Old Postage Stamps and More!

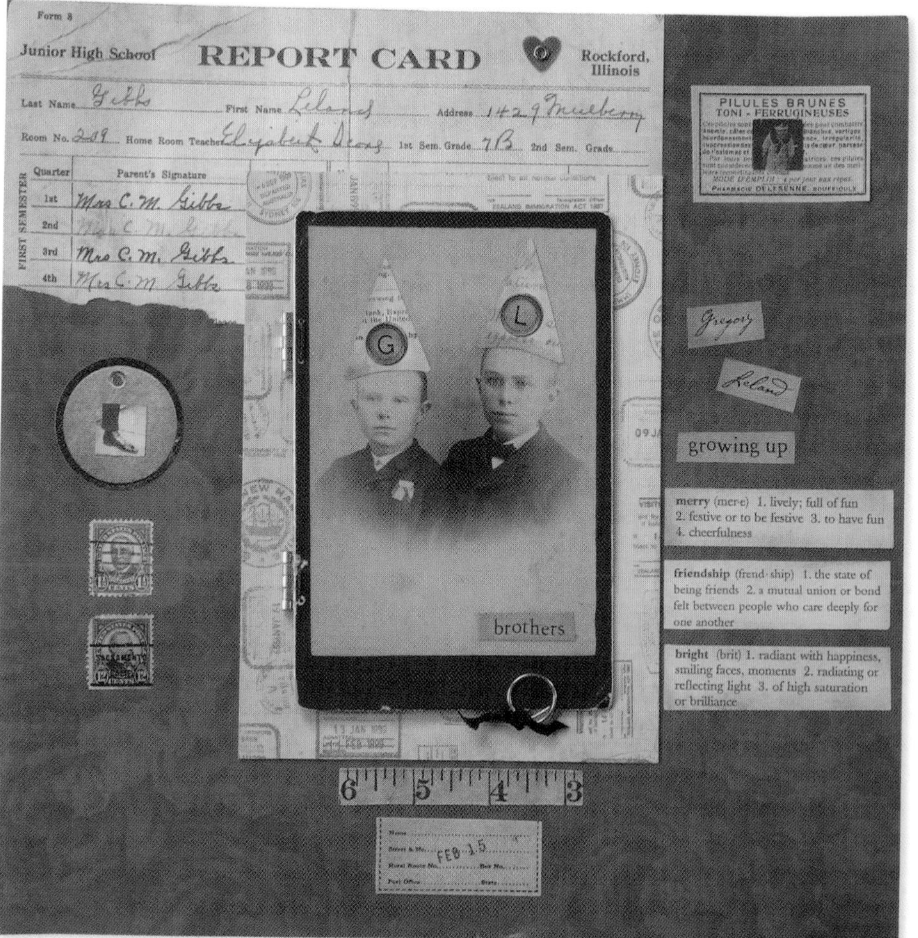

Assemble Page

1. Adhere ruler strips to page.

2. Age page with glazes and chalking ink.

3. Stamp titles on Space Saver.

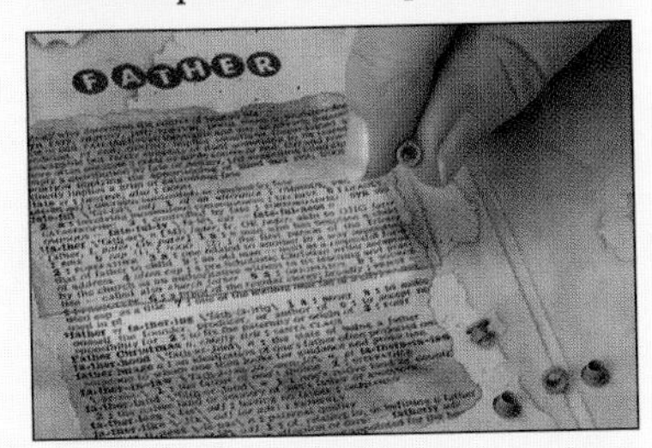

4. Attach microscope slides to Space Saver with eyelets.

5. String tags with descriptive words on thread.

DEFINING ARNOLD

by Mary Kaye Seckler

MATERIALS: *Design Originals* Legacy Collage Paper (#0547 Dictionary) • Plum & Cream cardstock • *Kinetic Scrapbooking* White Four-Way Space Saver • *PSX* Buttons rubber stamp alphabet set • *Marvy* Brown ink pad • *ColorBox* Chestnut Cat's Eye chalking ink • *Golden* Burnt Umber glaze • *Sonnets* scrapbook stickers • *McGill* 1/8" circle and rectangle punches • *Scrappy's* gold metal corners • *Foofala* plastic microscope slides • Gold brads • 12 White tags • *On the Surface* Plum metallic thread • *Tombow* Mono Multi Liquid Glue • *Hermafix* Temporary Bond • Dictionary definitions • 1/8" Gold eyelets

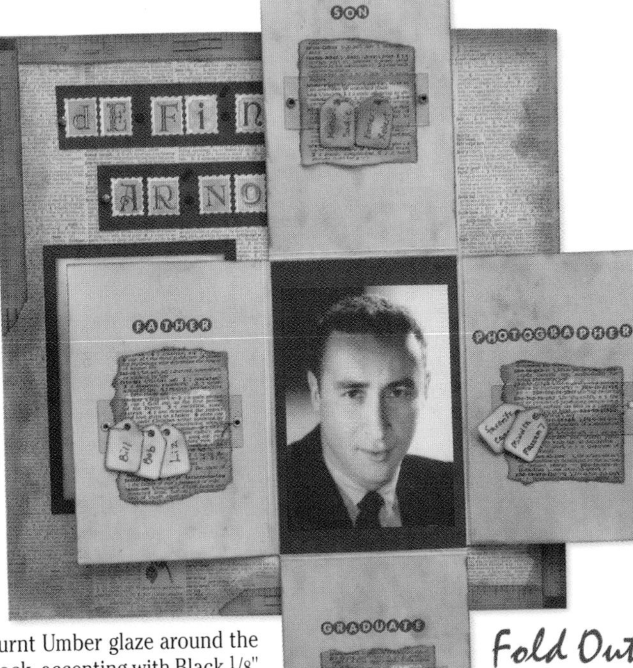

Fold Out Flaps for More Photos!

INSTRUCTIONS: Glue torn ruler pieces to Dictionary paper. • Age paper with Burnt Umber glaze around the edges, then edge with Chestnut chalking ink. • Affix letter stickers to Plum cardstock, accenting with Black 1/8" circles and rectangles. • Trim Plum cardstock frame to size; adhere to the top left of the scrapbook page using a temporary bond. (I use temporary bond on many elements in case I need to reposition.) • Set Gold eyelets in title bar. • Spritz a strong coffee solution on both sides of Space Saver. Cover the cardstock completely and allow the coffee to puddle in places. • Add instant coffee crystals while the paper is wet to enhance the antiqued look. • Coffee dye a dozen 1" White tags at the same time. Allow the papers to dry thoroughly. • Copy appropriate definitions; tear out. • Age with Burnt Umber glaze and Chestnut chalking ink. • Adhere definitions to center of each panel. • Stamp the words in Brown ink. • Punch 1/8" hole on ends of plastic microscope slides, affix to panel over definition with eyelets.(Note: if you are using both sides of panels, prepare the definitions for both sides of a panel to be sure they line up properly. Then set a slide on each side using the same two eyelets.) • Write details like 'Father' on tags; string tags through eyelets. • Mat photos and adhere to panels. • Mount packet to page.

TIME ACCORDION FOLD BOOK

by Carol Wingert

MATERIALS: *Design Originals* Legacy Collage Paper (#0528 Watches) • *Paper Bliss* textured bookboard for covers • *Ellison* die-cut Negative Image • *7 gypsies* watch face • *Making Memories* eyelet brad & eyelet flower • *Stampers Anonymous* word charm • *EK Success* Rebecca Sower Designs Tiny Letter Tag • *Coffee Break Designs* Mini Copper frames & eyelets • *Limited Edition* scrabble letters • *ColorBox* aging ink & chalking ink • *Tsukineko* Brilliance ink • *Hero Arts* Alphabet rubber stamps • *Lumiere* paint • *Designs by Pamela* Silver charm • Hemp • PVA glue • Bone folder

INSTRUCTIONS: Cut a $2^1/4$" x 12" piece of Watches paper. • Fold accordion book following instructions on page 7. • Add mini photos, quotes and embellishments. • Hand-journal if desired. • Age and embellish front cover. • Place hemp or ribbon in the middle of the back of the front and back covers to create ties. • Secure to the cover backs. • Adhere back of first accordion panel to back of front cover and back of last accordion panel to back of back cover with PVA glue. • Place weight on top of book until dry.

ACCORDION FOLD INSERTS FOR BOOKS;

1. Determine how many accordion panels you desire for your book. (I use an even number of panels so that the book is flat when completely open.) Also, determine what the finished size of each panel will be. This will determine what size sheet of paper you will need to create the insert. Mini books may be created out of 12" x 12" sheets of cardstock or text paper. (See mini book sample using collage paper.)

2. Cut paper into the correct size strip. For example: You want an eight-panel accordion fold with each panel being 5" x 7". You will need a 40" x 7" strip of paper. Cut with a long metal ruler and X-Acto knife.

3. Fold paper in half. Burnish the fold with a bone folder.

4. Fold each panel in half again, toward the valley centerfold. Burnish with bone folder.

5. Fold the top panels back to the end mountain folds. Burnish.

6. Fold the last sections back to the center fold. Burnish.

7. Your folds are now complete. Fold accordion style.

***Contrary to popular belief, this method is the most accurate for creating panels of equal size. Measuring and folding each panel individually often creates panels of slightly differing sizes. This comes from inaccuracies in measuring which may be as small as fractions of an inch.

Assemble Tags Book

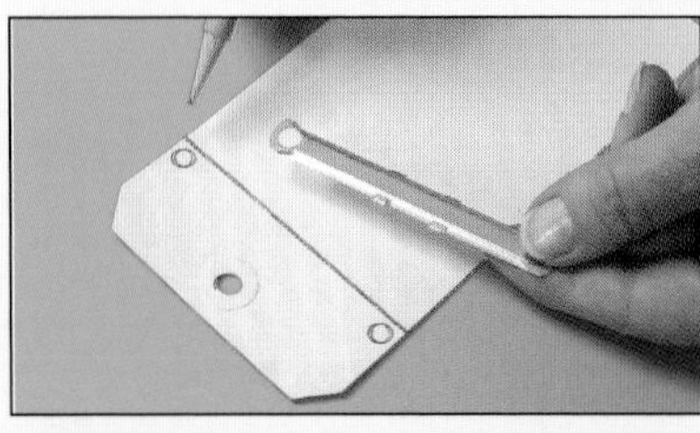

1. Score a line 1" from end of tag. Place slide portion of fastener against line and mark and punch holes.

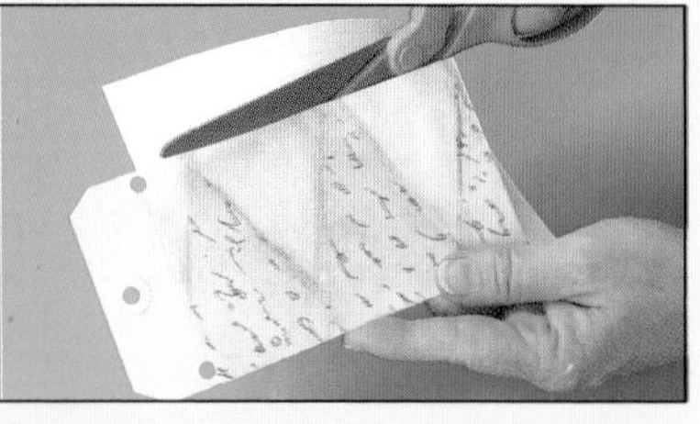

2. Cover tags with decorative paper and trim.

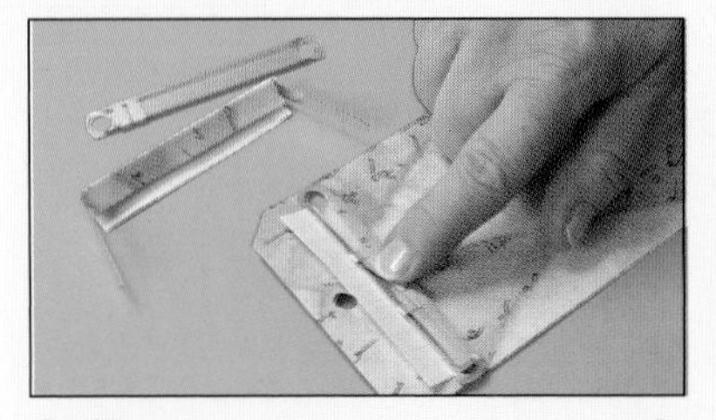

3. Place prong in tag; cover with decorative paper.

4. Embellish front cover and age with chalks.

FAMILY TAGS BOOK *by Delores Frantz*

MATERIALS: *Design Originals* Legacy Collage Papers (#0526 Two Ladies, #0546 Currency) • Four $3^1/4$" x $6^1/4$" tags • *ColorBox* Chestnut Roan Cat's Eye chalking ink • Metal rimmed tags • Metal file fastener • Flat marble • Metal letter tiles • 2 star nailheads • Vellum • Twine • Adhesive

INSTRUCTIONS: Score a line 1" from end of tag. Place slide portion of fastener against line and mark and punch holes. • For a six-page booklet, score and punch 4 tags. • For front and back cover, completely cover both sides of 2 tags. Re-punch holes. • For inside pages, cover both sides of tags just a little past score lines, leaving the punched holes uncovered. Tip: Glue tag to paper then cut around tag. • Age edges of covered tags. • Cut two 1"x $2^3/4$" pieces of paper. Wrap one piece around prong portion of fastener and glue to secure. • Stack pages, thread prongs through holes from front to back. Thread slide portion on prongs. • Place other small piece of paper under slide. Bend prongs down and secure with slides. Fold paper over fastener and glue to secure. • Embellish front cover. • Cover mini tags with paper. Use chalk to color tag strings. • Add stars and attach to booklet. • Glue photos to pages. • Journal on vellum and glue under pictures.

T
IMPORTANT.
together
Moments go by
Life is a succession of moments. To live each one is to succeed.
-Corita Kent
FAMILY
Eau de
9, Rue de la Paix
PARIS
Byrd, Claude, Virginia, Billy Clay & Delores
Granny Byrd
Delores & Billy Clay
Chloe, Claude, Byrd, Delores & Billy Clay
Claude & Delores
Mary, Tansy, Chloe, Al, Granny Byrd & Delores
Turn the Tag Book Vertically to Open the Pages... Wonderful Vintage Photos Make This Little Book Really Special!

Beth Cote

Beth is a professional artist who works with mixed media and book art. Beth designed the fabulous Legacy Collage Papers for Scrapbooking, Altered Art, Cards and Home Decor. Her focus is Altered Books. She travels across the country teaching popular paper arts workshops at retreats, shops and conventions.

Beth's teaching schedule and altered book ideas are on her Web site at www.alteredbook.com or email her at cacote@aeroinc.net

Carol Wingert **Mary Kaye Seckler** **Katrina Hogan**

Clock parts in a niche.

A little bottle in a box.

Dice and memorabilia.

A button and a key.

BEDTIME

by Tim Holtz

MATERIALS: *Design Originals* Legacy Collage Papers (#0534 Ruth's Violets, #0541 Report Card) • *Ranger* Coffee archival ink • *Petersen Arne* vellum and kraft cardstock • *Making Memories* eyelets, brads & letters • *US ArtQuest* mica tiles • *Crafter's Pick* Memory Mount & The Ultimate! • Foam Core • Found objects • Metal ruler • Craft knife

INSTRUCTIONS: Cut photos to size for page. • Mark areas on page for windows. • Create windows for page in foam core and Ruth's Violets paper. • Add Report Card paper to back of foam core. • Tear cardstock for photo mat and apply Coffee ink using direct to paper. • Add strips of paper to mat and secure with eyelets. • Glue photo to mat and then to Ruth's Violets paper with Memory Mount. • Print text on vellum and secure to page with eyelets. • Add title to inside top niche using metal letters and brads. • Glue small ink bottle, feather, pen nib, clock face and mica embellishments to window using The Ultimate! adhesive.

SUPPLIERS - Most craft and variety stores carry an excellent assortment of supplies. If you need something special, ask your local store to contact the following companies:

Legacy & Legacy Collage Papers, Slide Mounts & Transparency Sheets
Design Originals
www.d-originals.com
800-877-7820
2425 Cullen Street, Ft.Worth, Tx 76107

ColorBox Cat's Eye by Clearsnap
800-448-4862
PO Box 18, Anacortes, WA 98221

Golden Artist Colors
800-959-6543
188 Bell Road, New Berlin, NY 13411

7 gypsies
www.7gypsies.com
800-588-6707
440 S. Val Vista #56, Mesa, AZ 85204

Jacquard Products
distributed by US ArtQuest
800-200-7848
7800 Ann Arbor Rd., Grass Lake, MI 49240

Postmodern Design Stamps
405-321-3176
PO Box 720416, Norman, OK 73070

MANY THANKS to my friends for their cheerful help and wonderful ideas!
Kathy McMillan • Jennifer Laughlin
Janet Long • Janie Ray
David & Donna Thomason